GEORGES ROUAULT

THE MUSEUM OF MODERN ART

PAINTINGS AND PRINTS

GEORGES ROUAULT

BY JAMES THRALL SOBY

CONTENTS

ACKNOWLEDGMENTS

I should like to acknowledge the gracious assistance of Alfred H. Barr, Jr., René Batigne, Mrs. Florence Paull Berger, Joseph Brummer, Parker Tyler Davis, Miss Una E. Johnson, Philipp Loewenfeld, Pierre Matisse, Miss Agnes Mongan, Dr. Grace L. McCann Morley, Charles Nagel, Jr., J. B. Neumann, John O'Connor, Jr., Walter Pach, Duncan Phillips, John Rewald, Daniel Catton Rich, Miss Agnes Rindge, Andrew C. Ritchie, John S. Thacher, Miss Elise Van Hook, Gordon Washburn and Monroe Wheeler.

I am particularly indebted to Mr. and Mrs. Robert Woods Bliss, Sam A. Lewisohn, Lt. James S. Plaut, U.S.N.R., Carl O. Schniewind, James Johnson Sweeney, Curt Valentin and Lionello Venturi— all of whom have been of active and invaluable help in assembling the exhibition.

JAMES THRALL SOBY,
Director of the Exhibition.

LENDERS

Mr. and Mrs. Walter C. Arensberg, Hollywood; Mr. and Mrs. R. Kirk Askew, Jr., New York; Lt. and Mrs. Lee A. Ault, New Canaan, Conn.; Dr. and Mrs. Harry Bakwin, New York; Max Bangerter, Paris; Mr. and Mrs. Ralph M. Coe, Cleveland; Mr. and Mrs. Ralph F. Colin, New York; Mme. Marie Cuttoli, Paris; Werner Feuz, Clarens, Switzerland; Marcel Fleischmann, Zurich; Dr. Girardin, Paris; Mr. and Mrs. Vladimir Golschmann, New York; Jean Goriany; Leonard C. Hanna, Jr., Cleveland; Dr. and Mrs. MacKinley Helm, Brookline, Mass.; Miss Marion G. Hendrie, Cincinnati; Dr. F. H. Hirschland, Harrison, N. Y.; Frank B. Hubachek, Chicago; R. Sturgis Ingersoll, Philadelphia; Miss Mary E. Johnston, Glendale, Ohio; Mr. and Mrs. Sam A. Lewisohn, New York; Lt. Wright Ludington, Santa Barbara, Calif.; Mme. Carlos Martins, Washington, D. C.; Mr. and Mrs. Samuel A. Marx, Chicago; Lt. Henry P. McIlhenny, U.S.N.R., Philadelphia; Walter Pach, New York; Lt. and Mrs. Joseph Pulitzer, Jr., St. Louis; Bernard J. Reis, New York; Miss Ann C. Resor, Greenwich, Conn.; Miss Helen L. Resor, Greenwich, Conn.; Elmer Rice, Stamford, Conn.; Miss Agnes Rindge, Poughkeepsie, N. Y.; Miss Mary Rumsey, New York; Albert Sarraut, Paris; Mr. and Mrs. Carl O. Schniewind, Chicago; Mme. Henry Simon, Paris; Mr. and Mrs. Maurice Sterne, Mount Kisco, N. Y.; Mrs. Dudley Thayer, Weisel, Pa.; Lionello Venturi, New York; Glenway Westcott, Hampton, N. J.; Mr. and Mrs. Samuel S. White, III, Ardmore, Pa.

The Buffalo Fine Arts Academy, Albright Art Gallery; The Art Institute of Chicago; Wadsworth Atheneum, Hartford; The Brooklyn Museum, New York; Carnegie Institute, Pittsburgh; The Portland Art Museum, Ore.; The Dumbarton Oaks Research Library and Collection, Harvard University, Washington, D. C.; Phillips Memorial Gallery, Washington, D. C.

Bignou Gallery; Buchholz Gallery; Pierre Matisse Gallery; Perls Galleries; Weyhe Gallery; all in New York.

GEORGES ROUAULT: PAINTINGS AND PRINTS

Georges Rouault: a solitary figure in an era of group manifestoes and shared directions; a devout Catholic and devotional painter in a period when artists more often have run the gamut of anti-religious feeling, from indifference to irreverence; a painter of sin and redemption in the face of prevailing estheticism and counter-estheticism; an artist with a limited vision of unlimited ferocity in contrast to many other leading painters who have scanned and pivoted but seldom stared fixedly for long; a man who has opposed Henri-Matisse's peaceful wish that art evoke "the same sensation as a good armchair," by making much of his own painting resemble a seat of moral judgment. Thus—Rouault since the early years of his career, which began in the 1890s.

We now tend to revere him, perhaps with undue emphasis, for his solitary position in modern French art, and there are those who, disliking 20th century painting in general, speak of him as Jacques Maritain has spoken of Léon Bloy, Rouault's spiritual master in youth—"a Job on the dung-hill of modern culture."[1] Others would apply to Rouault the artist's equivalent words on Bloy: "He vomits his epoch."[2] Yet Rouault belongs to the contemporary tradition in many important respects: he won attention with the Fauve generation of 1905; his work is unthinkable without the precedent of the Post-Impressionists in art and of the late 19th century Catholic writers, especially Léon Bloy, in literature.

In this country we tend, too, to think of Rouault as breaking through to fame in recent years—a dark horse of the modern movement.

Yet his work was fully appreciated here before the First World War by a small group of collectors and critics, some of whom probably had seen one or both of his exhibitions at the Galerie Druet, Paris, in 1910 and 1911. Certainly the penitent psychology of wartime has increased the regard in which he is held, and in terms of popular acclaim a recent writer was justified in saying "his pictures seem to have been reserved for a generation that is capable of a tragic vision."[3] But Rouault's fame rests on surer ground than non-conformity and sudden psychological accord with the times. Viewed less emotionally, in relation to other living artists, he emerges as one of the few major figures in 20th century painting.

Childhood; Apprenticeship in the Hirsch Workshop

"In reality," Jacques Maritain has written, "he [Rouault] belongs in the category of the shy explosives. Parisian through his mother, but Celtic and Breton through his father . . . ."[4] The artist was born in Paris on May 27, 1871, during the bombardment of the city by the *Versaillais* of the Commune, a bombardment which is said to have forced his mother to take refuge in the cellar of her house and hastened her labor. Rouault's birth amid the terror of exploding shells inevitably has been hailed as an augury of his distraught painting. A less romantic but perhaps more pertinent fact is that he grew up under the affectionate eye of a grandfather who admired Callot, Rembrandt, Courbet, Manet and owned lithographs by Daumier. Rouault himself has paid tribute to his grandfather's influence: "As a child face to face with reality, I went first to the school of Daumier, before knowing Raphael . . . My grandfather walked the quais in search of various reproductions of paintings he liked. Daumier formed the nucleus of his modest purchases."[5] This grandfather desperately wanted Rouault to become an artist. The boy began by becoming a craftsman (his father was employed in the Pleyel piano factory as a wood finisher). At fourteen he was sent to the stained glass maker, Hirsch, as an apprentice.

What kind of stained glass did Rouault make or repair? Did his work in the Hirsch studio influence his mature style as an artist? To the first of these questions there is no available answer beyond Rouault's own statement: "I have been told before that my painting reminded people of stained glass. That's probably because of my original trade . . . My work consisted in supervising the firing, and sorting the little pieces of glass that fell out of the windows they brought us to repair. This latter task inspired me with an enduring passion for old stained glass."[6] And though the second question would seem to be answered, too, by this statement of the artist, it is still argued variously. Certain critics hold that the influence of Rouault's apprenticeship has been negligible in his work. In support of this theory it has been pointed out that those aspects of his technique which most resemble that of stained glass windows—his juxtapositions of smoldering reds, blues and greens and his use of heavy, "leaded" contours—were not adopted until many years after his association with Hirsch, following a decade or more during which he worked in a quite different style.

This argument seems unconvincing for several reasons. First of all, more than one painter has reverted to childhood inspiration or adolescent experience at precisely the moment when he has attained maturity as an artist, *after* a period of groping in which earlier memory played no direct part. (The paintings which Rouault completed in Moreau's studio, though extraordinarily competent, can scarcely be considered mature by comparison with his later work.) Secondly, it seems logical that Rouault, perhaps unconsciously, should have begun to draw on the memory of Gothic windows at the time when he was psychologically and emotionally swayed by the personality and writings of the impassioned champion of the Middle Ages, Léon Bloy. But this all-important spiritual alliance did not reach its climax until late 1903 or early 1904, when Rouault read Bloy's novel, *La Femme Pauvre*. Shortly afterward, his sonorous blues and reds began to take on a Gothic intensity. He did not use heavy, black contours until several years later, but the relation of these contours to window leading seems apparent. (Though these contours are no more dense and assertive than those which Henri-Matisse used from 1906 to 1908, their function appears divisional rather than primarily rhythmic as with Matisse.) And finally, it was Rouault himself who once said: "I do not feel as if I belong to this modern life on the streets where we are walking at this moment; my real life is back in the age of the cathedrals."[7] For a colorist like Rouault, the age of the cathedrals must have been above all a time of incredibly rich alchemy in glass.

If we grant the point of resemblance between 12th and 13th century windows and Rouault's color and outline in certain paintings, there remains a third interrelation which deserves mention, though here we are dealing with conjecture rather than almost certain fact. This is the Gothic distortion of form in a few paintings such as the *Clownerie* (page 70) of c. 1917, in which the figures seem bowed to an imaginary arch. Moreover, there are certain other pictures of this period, notably the *Crucifixion* (page 71),

6

which are so rigidly frontal and vertical in composition as to suggest those center panels around which Gothic windows rose to their peaked tension of design. (Subject matter aside, it is not at all difficult to imagine *Clownerie* as a planned foil to the *Crucifixion*.) The wry-necked stylization of the figures in Rouaults of the middle period may, of course, have derived from other sources. It was common in the paintings of his master, Gustave Moreau; it fascinated Rouault in Ingres' *Roger and Angelica* of which he has spoken so often—"Ingres' Angelica, with its long neck stylized like an antique column transported to an evil place."[8] But it may after all be one more indication of the importance of Rouault's early years as an apprentice in Hirsch's studio where so much medieval glass was brought for repair.

The Ecole des Beaux-Arts: Gustave Moreau

For several years, while he was working with Hirsch, Rouault attended evening classes at the *Ecole Nationale des Arts Décoratifs*, where he executed the *Nude* (right) and where he may have acquired the interest in ceramics which was later to develop so brilliantly (pages 58 and 59). In 1891 he enrolled in the *Ecole des Beaux-Arts* under Elie Delaunay, to whom Gustave Moreau succeeded the following year. Rouault, as is well known, became Moreau's favorite pupil, and shortly after the latter's death in 1898 was named Director of the *Musée Gustave Moreau*, a post he retains to this day.

The sympathetic relationship between master and pupil seems surprising at first glance, since Moreau was a specialist in that elaborate and sumptuous detail which he described as "necessary richness," while Rouault was later to declare: "Painting is summed up in so few essential traits."[9] Yet the philosophical bonds between the two were extraordinarily close. For

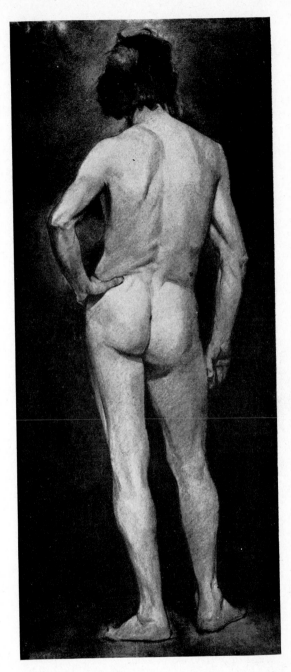

Nude. c. 1890. Collection the artist (?). Not in the exhibition.

Moreau was a late-life child of Romanticism, a medievalist, devoted to moral sentiments and opposed to superficial reality in art whether based upon nature (Courbet's realism) or science (Impressionism). The master apparent-

The Prodigal Son. c. 1892. Collection the artist.
Not in the exhibition.

ly often lectured his pupils on the need for a deeper inspiration than that provided by the tangible and the real, since "without such an attachment painting could never blossom as it had in the Middle Ages."[10] The eagerness with which Rouault listened to such advice can easily be understood. Moreover, the Expressionist basis of Rouault's mature art is prefigured in Moreau's statement that "Art is a furious tracking down of the inner feelings solely by means of plastic expression."[11]

By the testimony of numerous distinguished pupils, Moreau was a gifted and tolerant teacher—"The Animator, that is his genius and name," André Suarès has said of him.[12] Unlike most academicians of the period, he stressed the importance of color, a fact which must have endeared him to an instinctive colorist like Rouault. And certainly it was from Moreau

that Rouault learned much of the secret of that nacre of tone which distinguishes so many of the latter's works. It was from him that Rouault learned to admire Rembrandt with an enduring passion—a passion so fierce in its early stages that it appears to have worried Moreau. "One day," Rouault relates, "G. Moreau and I stopped before the portrait of Rembrandt as an old man, in the *salon carré*. Pointing out the white bonnet in the background, he said to me that he feared I might become enslaved . . . I replied: 'I would rather be enslaved all my life by Rembrandt than get myself up in the fashion of the day which does not suit me at all.'"[13] The preference is amply confirmed by *The Quarry* (page 34) of 1897.

Under Moreau's tutelage Rouault painted several large pictures which are clearly dominated by the conventions of his master's studio, though they are evidence of a first-rate and even precocious talent (left). Only one of these large paintings, *The Ordeal of Samson* (page 33), is available for the exhibition. Completed in 1893 and entered unsuccessfully on Moreau's advice for the *Prix de Rome*, it contains a clue to Rouault's later style in the handling of the face of the soldier with upraised arm in the right foreground. The harsh grimace of this face is amply precedented in both Italian and Northern art of the late 15th and early 16th centuries. It is, however, slightly out of key with the less impassioned conception of Rouault's composition as a whole. It suggests, if inconclusively, the direction in which he was going, a direction in which it might be necessary to forget esthetics, in a measure, in order to remember Faith.

Years later Rouault wrote: "When, toward 1894, I painted my *Infant Jesus Among the Doctors* [which won him the *Prix Chénavard*], almost no one spoke of religious art."[14] He himself at that time aspired only to paint religious subjects, not to achieve a religious art of inner compulsion. But his ambition was soon to in-

Self Portrait. 1899. Pencil drawing. Collection the artist. Not in the exhibition.

Self Portrait. c. 1896. Oil. Collection the artist. Not in the exhibition.

tensify, and perhaps Moreau's death in 1898 averted a break between master and pupil over the role which religion should play in art. To Moreau, religion was an iconographical storehouse; to Rouault it was soon to become the sum—or very nearly the sum—of personal experience and emotion. The introspective deepening of the young artist's character is revealed by a comparison of two self portraits: the one conventionally romantic (above right); the other as searching and personal a document as many drawings by Vincent van Gogh (above left). (At this period Rouault is said to have made innumerable drawings of his own nose and mouth, seen in a mirror.) In his quest for a more profound expression of his rising religious conviction, Rouault found inspiration in the work of two of the most impassioned Catholic writers

of late 19th century France—Ernest Hello (1828–1885) and, above all, Léon Bloy (1846–1917) who became for a time a close personal friend and mentor.

Early Landscapes; Forain; the Influence of Hello's and Bloy's Philosophies

From 1898 to 1902 Rouault, separated from his family and bitterly unhappy, painted a number of lugubrious landscapes in the pervading blue tonality used by so many artists of our century during their formative years. But he had not forgotten the anti-academic impression made by a Forain drawing which he had seen in youth, an impression he himself has described: "When art was for me the Promised Land (and

9

until death it always will be) Forain, with a black and white drawing, aroused in the child I was then, a gleam, an inward perception of a rare thing . . . which, after the chore of 'drawing well' in my evening class, gave me hope . . . I lacked means of expression; I was ignorant; but I had a secret instinct which told me that here was a living source . . ."[15]

In 1903 his "secret instinct" found expression in mature terms after a serious illness but more particularly as a result of his friendship with Léon Bloy. He became devoutly religious and adopted the dictum of Bloy's spokesman, Marchenoir, in *La Femme Pauvre*: "If art does not go on its knees, . . . it must necessarily go on its back or its belly."[16] To a convert like Rouault (and it should be remembered that as a child he had attended Protestant schools for a time), the depth of Bloy's faith must have been singularly impressive. Bloy's life had been a continuous anguish of poverty and disappointment, yet the concluding line of *La Femme Pauvre*, spoken by its martyred heroine, Clotilde, summarizes his persuasion: "There is only one grief —not to be a saint."[17]

Since the relationship between Bloy and Rouault hereafter is dealt with at some length, it seems only fair to preface what follows with Rouault's own words of disclaimer: "Certain people have linked me with him [Bloy], the critics followed them like Panurge's sheep, and I became the *Léon Bloy of painting* without having wished or sought it."[18] Nevertheless, it was after meeting Bloy, after reading his *Le Désespéré* ("for a long time I had with me the original of 'Désespéré' "[19]) and later after reading *La Femme Pauvre*, that Rouault prepared to earn the title, "the monk of painting in our time,"[20] and to develop that devout and tragic art which was to prompt André Suarès to write to him: "You paint as one exorcises."[21]

But wherein does a religious painter differ from a painter of religious subjects? In broad terms the answer is self-evidently a matter of heartfelt conviction as opposed to surface interest. But such an answer does not take into account the passion of the Catholicism practiced by Hello and Bloy, nor does it reflect their desire for a drastic reform of all the arts. Let Hello, who died when Rouault was a child, speak first: "Art," he wrote, "is one of the forces which have corrupted the imagination, because art has said that evil was beautiful. Art must be one of the forces which will cure the imagination; it must say that evil is ugly."[22] (One thinks immediately of Rouault's paintings of prostitutes.) Further, Hello believed that art and religion were absolutely inseparable: "Religion and art live in the same atmosphere, both colored by the same far reflections, both dishonored by the same turpitudes."[23] He inveighed against those painters and critics who considered the martyrdom of Saint Sebastian a gracious vehicle for technical display. The function of art, he declared, was to tell the truth— the religious truth. This, indeed, was art's particular responsibility, for "when the mediocre man, describing a lie, uses the phrase '*this is poetic*,' he thinks he has relieved the liar of blame. On the contrary, he has made a new accusation, for if the liar lies *poetically*, he falsifies words in their highest form."[24]

In Bloy's books, Hello's mystic conception of a truth-telling, healing art took on an apoplectic coloration of fleshly atonement. It has been said of him: "He was so concerned with the flesh that he magnified its importance down to its sediments by the play of analogies and symbolical figures. The ignoble furnished Bloy a continual theme for the exaltation of THAT which is the most opposed by definition to the flesh—the Holy Spirit."[25] And Bloy himself added: "I have yearned at this dreadful close of the century, when everything seems lost, to thrust at God the insistent outcry of dereliction and anxiety for the orphaned multitude which the Father in his celestial heights seems to be abandoning and which no longer has the strength even to die bravely."[26]

Clearly Rouault's approach to painting was strongly affected by the philosophy of Bloy which in turn was related to that of Hello. Yet as so often happens between literary men and painters (between Zola and Cézanne, for example), misunderstandings arose when Rouault began to follow the road Bloy had indicated. Bloy could not accept the projection in visual terms of a feverish conviction which so startlingly paralleled his own. He was able to admire the *Infant Christ Among the Doctors*, which Rouault had completed under Moreau's guidance, but when he visited the *Salon d'Automne* of 1905 and saw Rouault's intensely individual paintings, he wrote: "This is frightful. He is seeking a new direction, alas! This artist whom one would have believed capable of painting seraphim seems no longer to think of anything but atrocities and vengeful caricatures."[27] Two years later, after visiting the *Salon des Indépendants*, he wrote directly to the artist: "I still have two words to say to you, after which you will no longer be for me anything but a lost friend. First, you are exclusively interested in the ugly; you have a vertigo of hideousness. Secondly, if you were a man of prayer, a eucharist, an obedient soul, you could not paint these horrible canvases."[28]

Bloy's taste in painting was almost entirely formed by his religious conviction. A thorough Gothicist and reformer, he let his spokesman, Marchenoir in *La Femme Pauvre*, say for him, with more than Pre-Raphaelite vehemence: "Perhaps one day it will be possible to claim that the so-called religious painting of the men of the Renaissance has been no less disastrous for Christianity than Luther himself, and I await the *clairvoyant* poet who will sing the 'Paradise Lost' of our esthetic innocence."[29] And Marchenoir goes on to say: "A work of art

Portrait of Rupp. c. 1899. Collection the artist (?). Not in the exhibition.

which pretends to be religious but which does not evoke prayer is as monstrous as a beautiful woman who is uninspiring."[30]

Bloy and Rouault remained friends until the former's death in 1917, and Raïssa Maritain has written a touching description of the anguish their disagreement on painting cost Rouault— "How many times in the following years [after 1905] did we not see Rouault at Bloy's house, standing and leaning against the wall, with a slight smile on his closed lips, his gaze far off, his face apparently impassive but with a pallor that increased when the question of modern painting was broached. Rouault grew ever more pale, but kept an heroic silence to the end. . . . It seemed as if he sought from Bloy the very

11

indictments which tormented within him that which he held most dear. . . ."[31]

There was no possibility of an understanding between the two men. For though Rouault's works of 1903–1907 lacked completely the beguiling grace which Bloy detested in Renaissance art, though they had the awful directness common to images from the age of "our esthetic innocence," they were not what Bloy was looking for. They were emphatically not paintings of seraphim. In the beginning of Rouault's mature career, they were often pictures of butchers passing through the rue de Fourneaux, clowns seen at the fête de Grenelle, destitute figures from the slums of Paris. Most often, they were pictures of the prostitutes of Paris and Versailles, recreated as monsters in the *camera obscura* of the artist's dreams.

1903-1904: The Paintings of Prostitutes

It is significant that many of the pictures which inaugurated Rouault's personal style should have reflected the frenzied preoccupation with sin and redemption expressed in Bloy's *Le Désespéré* and *La Femme Pauvre*. It seems likely, too, that Rouault's choice of prostitutes as symbols of earthly degradation—and also as subjects for instant redemption through suffering— was inspired by Bloy. Prostitutes had played a key part in Bloy's writing and life. He had loved and converted to his own passionate Catholicism two women of the streets, later used as heroines of his novels. (A parallel with the life of Vincent van Gogh is suggested.) In Bloy's novels, prostitutes are the absolute counterparts of saints, and he made abundantly clear that he was interested only in extremes of conduct and character.

Rouault's studies of prostitutes, executed in 1903 and 1904, are often in watercolor, which he used as a major medium throughout his early

career. It may have been watercolor which freed him from the elaborate chiaroscuro and brown tonality of his years in Moreau's studio and enriched the blue palette of his landscapes painted between 1898 and 1902. He worked now with summary directness, blocking in the forms with strong, anti-naturalistic highlights. The figures were sometimes spattered rather than modeled into existence, and he frequently used a broken-line technique which reappears in *Costumed Men* (page 35) which, though dated 1906, is close in style to the watercolors of 1903. The interiors which house his subjects are defined by a linear perspective which in later paintings was to be abandoned for an atmospheric manipulation of space through juxtaposed tones.

By comparison with such climactic paintings of prostitutes as the *Red-Haired Woman* (page 50), *Two Prostitutes* (page 44) and *The Sirens* (page 41), Rouault's watercolors of 1903–1904 preserve a certain detachment, a slightly picturesque flavor; the full force of his moral rebellion is not in them. A relation between these watercolors and Lautrec's art has been mentioned by several critics. But few of Rouault's early paintings show the sensual relish of decadence for its own satanic sake which characterized Lautrec's work. To Lautrec's cynicism, Rouault opposed tears and rage. He was not interested in the detailed decline of the flesh which so inevitably fascinated the crippled Lautrec. He sought the grimace and posture of irrevocable martyrdom. And he himself has indignantly denied the influence of the Degas-Lautrec tradition, explaining his change in direction as the result of a profound upheaval within himself—"I underwent then a moral crisis of the most violent sort. I experienced things which cannot be expressed by words. And I began to paint with an outrageous lyricism which disconcerted everybody. . . . It was not the influence of Lautrec, Degas or the moderns which inspired me, but an inner neces-

Léon Bloy. c. 1926. Lithograph. 9¼ x 6½".
Collection Jean Goriany.

Gustave Moreau (Moreau au Petit Chapeau).
1926 (?). Lithograph, 9⅛ x 6¾". The Museum
of Modern Art, given anonymously,

sity and the perhaps unconscious desire not to
fall full-length into conventional religious subject matter."[32] And though the Degas-like
Woman with Red Stockings (page 38) would
seem to qualify this statement of the artist, the
picture appears isolated in his work and stands
in marked contrast to the severely personal
Woman with a Mirror (page 38).

The Salon d'Automne: Les Fauves

Rouault had exhibited in the *Salon* from 1895 to
1901, and from 1905 to 1912 showed annually
in the *Salon des Indépendants*. In 1902 and 1903
he helped found the *Salon d'Automne* which
opened the latter year. The current of religious
revival ran strong in the new organization: a

leading figure was Georges Desvallières who
dreamed of forming a school of painters under
the protection of Nôtre-Dame de Paris; one of
the *Salon's* founders was J. K. Huysmans whom
Rouault knew well and who, around 1901, had
tried to persuade him to enter the monastery at
Ligugé and there work in peace and retirement.
Huysmans' proposal must have appealed
strongly to the young artist, and it is likely that
it was rejected out of respect for the advice
which Moreau had given him previously. "If at
a certain moment," Rouault writes, "I felt the
need of going into retirement . . . he begged me
to stop and consider. 'You are young,' he said,
'in spite of your precocious experience in life.
You must live and learn to live in your own way,
not according to bookish theories . . . You must

not flee life so much; later on, in your decline or in advanced maturity, retirement may be possible.' "[33]

Perhaps the principal accomplishment of the new *Salon d'Automne* was on the one hand to reveal the full importance of the Post-Impressionist generation of Cézanne, on the other to give certain younger artists a place to exhibit their continuation of the explorations of Gauguin and van Gogh.

Some of these younger artists came to be known, in 1905, as the Fauves, and in that year Rouault's paintings were hung with theirs in the "Salon des Fauves" of the *Salon d'Automne*. He was never formally associated with the Fauve group, however, and his paintings caused a different scandal from theirs. The eight oils and thirty-two watercolors and pastels which he had exhibited in the *Salon d'Automne* of 1904 had created an impressive stir among critics and gallery goers, chiefly because of their blackness of tone. (One critic inquired whether his paintings of prostitutes were intended to represent Negresses in a tunnel.) The disreputable character of his subjects—weary clowns, mountebanks and pitchmen in addition to prostitutes—was naturally alarming to a public so lately won over to Monet's haystack and the rotund elegance of Renoir's Gabrielle, perhaps forgetful already of Daumier's *Scènes de Théâtre* and savage caricatures in terra cotta.

The paintings of both Rouault and the Fauves were Expressionist, a term usually defined as describing an art of inner vision as opposed to outer reality. But to the decorative Expressionism of Matisse, Derain, Friesz and the other Fauves, Rouault opposed a psychological Expressionism, sharper in emotion and more specific in protest. And while people disliked the flat, blazing patterns and linear distortions of the Fauves, this was after all a matter of *painting* and relatively free of disturbing subject. Following the triumph of the

Impressionists, the public was a little less dogmatic in its judgment of technical eccentricity, though no less vociferous, like an orator who shouts down the suspicion that he is developing the wrong points. But what was to be done with an artist who made *filles de joie* extraordinarily unjoyful, who painted clowns of beloved childhood memory as Pagliaccis too grieved to sob a note? The reply was what it has been so often for artists: the public abandoned Rouault's Expressionism to those few who could understand it, thus fulfilling Moreau's prophecy that his favorite pupil's career would be one of solitude and neglect.

Rouault nevertheless has steadfastly remained an Expressionist throughout his career, though in lessening degree. He himself has indirectly accepted the classification. "Subjective artists are one-eyed," he has said, "but objective artists are blind."[34] He has disliked the elaborate intellectualism of 20th century art, and once dismissed it as "cerebral morphinomania."[35] He has declaimed against a dependence on surface reality—"as opposed to the reality which satisfied Renoir or Degas, I would say, almost as the Surrealists, that there exists on 'another plane' a very beautiful reality which is not that of the amateur photographer, who has always seen nature through the lens of his camera."[36] Like his younger contemporary, Giorgio de Chirico, who spoke of painting with his eyes closed, Rouault has felt the need of shutting out the world about him, and has written: "We have only to work like the deaf and the mute; for painters I hardly dare say like the blind. Nevertheless, it is sometimes good even for a painter to close his eyes for an instant."[37] The statement is significant in relation to Rouault's painting as a whole, but is foretold in Moreau's dictum: "I do not believe either in what I touch or what I see. I believe only in what I cannot see and in what I sense."[38]

1905-1906: The Climax of The Early Period

In his paintings of 1905 and 1906 Rouault's Expressionism reached a climax of ferocity and power, seldom to be attained—or attempted—in recent years. The basis of his technical procedure may be seen most clearly in the *Nude Torso* (page 39) in which there is the minimum intervention of subject matter. Here he has enveloped clear flat areas of broad highlight, recalling Cézanne in their transparency and tone, with strong shadows which contain the figure entirely and sometimes serve purely as emotional accents, without strict regard to source of light. But the *Nude Torso* is an "academy" piece—one of the few painted by Rouault since his student years, probably because his subjective premise would have obviated the use of models.* It is when the figure turns around, when she changes from model to prostitute or circus performer, that the full force of Rouault's Expressionism is felt, as in the *Prostitutes* in the Witzinger collection in Switzerland (page 40). Shadow is then used wherever and in whatever way it can add to the impact: it runs over the lighted areas with arbitrary abandon; it underlines the caricatural elements and sometimes defines them entirely; it ranges in density from outline to dominant mass.

In most Rouaults of this period, shadows are stained-glass blue and contours black, but these colors are used interchangeably, according to what Delacroix described as their "moral" value and what would now be described as their capacity for psychological implication. Thus, in the *Nude* (page 45)—a study for the *Two Prostitutes* of the following year—the blue of the

* It is interesting to note that Léon Bloy considered modeling the most degrading of all professions and once wrote: "The model's profession by contrast to prostitution leaves the woman completely destitute and divorces her from her personality, in order to relegate her to a limbo of black unconsciousness." (Léon Bloy, *La Femme Pauvre*, Paris, Mercure de France, 1937, p. 39.)

woman's hair is repeated in the shadows on the face, breast and thighs. Around the figure run the black trial contours which the artist has left uncorrected, like a spasmodic record of preliminary intention, adding to the unpremeditated vividness of the image. What is most important, Rouault's use of shadows and outlines seldom falls back upon formula. In the famous *Head of Christ* in the Chrysler collection, heavy lines are used as a virtual flagellation of the surface: a direct translation of the artist's emotion before the subject. Other paintings of the period, notably the *Circus* (cat. no. 15), show a balanced arrangement of opposing lights and darks, and the contours form a Baroque arabesque which is almost serene and certainly ordered. His placing of figures is nearly always masterly, and seems completely instinctive. "Design," he once remarked, "is a jet of the spirit on the alert."[39]

In *The Couple* (page 37), the *Woman at a Table* (page 45) and *Circus Woman* (page 43) emphasis is upon a caricatural grandeur which recalls Rouault's affinity to Goya and Forain which he has often acknowledged, his debt to Daumier to whom he paid passionate tribute in his *Souvenirs Intimes*, his regard for Félicien Rops whom he praised Huysmans for "discovering." Yet all three are highly original pictures, astonishing in their finality for a painter so recently arrived at a personal idiom. The single, defiant figure in *Circus Woman* is posed against a background of framed area and adjoining circus figures which are so handled as to suggest the Oriental wallpaper patterns of the Post-Impressionists. The figure itself is an unforgettable image, overwritten with the artist's furious energy and daring. Its malignance is a little surprising in a circus subject, since Rouault appears to have admired clowns for their itinerant detachment from worldly affairs, their status as melancholy witnesses of bourgeois corruption, their intense privacy and specialization

15

of professional life. His clowns often weep for humanity; they seldom accuse it as they do in *Circus Woman* and one or two additional paintings of the early period.

The Sirens (page 41), the *Two Prostitutes* (page 44), the *Red-Haired Woman* (page 50) and the *Prostitutes* (page 40) represent high points in the series devoted to this subject. In the last-named picture, as in the *Odalisque* of 1907 (page 48), the Post-Impressionists' admiration for Japanese prints is again reflected in the flat, calligraphic treatment and economy of line used for the background figures. But the two foreground figures in *Prostitutes* are the absolute opposite of decoration *à la Japonaise*. They stand, monumental in accusation, like figures of nightmare remorse. Yet Maritain's words on Bloy apply equally to Rouault—"His invective was aimed, in fact, at something different from the apparent target."[40]

Paintings 1907-1909

By the end of 1906 Rouault had developed a good part of the iconography upon which he has drawn throughout his subsequent career. He had explored landscape, *maisons closes*, the theatre, the circus and religious subjects. He had developed an Expressionist art of perhaps greater intensity than any painter since van Gogh. It may have been as a respite from so emotionally consuming an accomplishment, that he turned in 1906–1907 to paintings of bathers—a subject for which Cézanne had reserved much of his proudest ambition. The year 1907 also marks a point of closer contact between Rouault and the Fauves, particularly Matisse, who was then applying the lessons of Cézanne to his own purpose. But it seems certain that Rouault went direct to Cézanne's painting for inspiration. The effect of Cézanne's color had been felt in the rose, blue and orange tones of Rouault's watercolors of 1903–1905, as previously mentioned. In 1907, however, his

bathers revealed his concern with the formalist element in Cézanne, with the interrelation of more or less abstract volumes which had so engrossed the master of Aix and so separately influenced the Fauves and the Cubists.

The logical forerunners of Rouault's bathers are a few paintings of 1907 in which his prostitutes are turned into odalisques, still harsh in feature but more sensuous in body and more carefully composed in relation to the setting in which they recline (page 48). From these odalisques he may have progressed naturally to the open-air bather scenes whose subjects are balanced against light and landscape and are free of the emotional tension and moral significance of his 1906 studies of prostitutes.

Only two of his bather subjects, a watercolor and an oil, are available for this publication (pages 48 and 49). Even allowing for the difference in medium, the two pictures are quite different in character. While the watercolor seems related to the watercolors of Cézanne's later career (though also close in its simple, rhythmic energy to Matisse's *Bather* of c. 1908 in the Museum's Collection), the oil is conceived in much the same spirit as those Baroque paintings of nudes in landscape which Cézanne completed in the 1870s. Both Rouault's paintings, however, are pointed toward a calculated compositional order. Taken together they contribute evidence of the dual nature of his inheritance as an artist: on the one hand Expressionism and the satirical precedent of Goya, Daumier, Rops and Forain; on the other the example of Cézanne's attempt to re-do Poussin after nature. Rouault himself has proposed a monument to commemorate this inheritance. "At Marseilles," he has written, "I have dreamed of a glorious triptych to the memory of Puget, Cézanne and Daumier, to be placed at the end of the Avenue Pierre-Puget—a favorable and ready-made place."[41]

The years 1907–1909 furnish particularly emphatic proof of Rouault's dual preoccupation during his early career. To the bathers of that period are opposed several heads of clowns (pages 46 and 47) in which both the Baroque and the classical tendencies of Cézanne's early and late periods respectively are abandoned in favor of a portraiture of great psychological penetration and deliberately narrowed focus. The balanced areas of wash color used in his *Bathers* watercolor have been replaced by a slashing impasto in oil, the contrapuntal arrangement of abstracted forms condensed to the close-up of a single image. The color is lighter and more glowing than ever before; the overwriting of broad brushstrokes more structural and controlled than in the works of 1905–1906. The facial make-up of the clowns is freely altered for a subjective emphasis which reaches a high point in the powerful *Make-Up, Cirque Forain* (page 56) of 1911. Rouault has been one of the few modern artists for whom the human head has proved continuously inspiring. In his own words, "at a time when the human visage represented for certain artists only the type of official Salon portrait and for others held little interest, I found it an infinite and incomparably rich source of means of expression."[42]

Perhaps in the clowns' heads of 1907 and 1908 we are at the beginning of that interest in the sensuous qualities of pigment which has developed steadily in Rouault's work, culminating in figure pieces of the late 1930s such as *The Last Romantic* (page 87) and *The Old King* (color frontispiece) and also in very recent still lifes (page 89). But it would be dangerous to attempt to chart Rouault's development in precise chronological terms. His method of working has been unconventional, though used by certain artists of the past, among them the American Romantic, Albert Pinkham Ryder. He has begun a number of paintings at a given period and finished them separately at intervals of many years, with widely varying alterations and additions. The method is in marked contrast to that of many modern artists who work each picture through to its final state under the impetus of a continuous and specific inspiration. It is opposite to the system of painting successive series of canvases which men like Picasso and (surprisingly) Miro have adopted. Rouault's system has obviously suited him well and has only occasionally led him to staleness or confusion of style. But it is a method which discourages chronological analysis.

Around 1907 Rouault began several satirical paintings of judges whom he presents, in a critic's apt phrase, as "between the bear and the ass."[43] Judges were for him, as they had been for Daumier, symbols of bourgeois corruption, of justice become a travesty of itself through the callousness of the prosperous middle classes. And if Daumier and Forain furnish the most conspicuous precedent for Rouault's satire on judges, it is significant that Léon Bloy had saved the most violent passages in that extraordinarily violent book, *La Femme Pauvre*, for a condemnation of the bourgeoisie and its officialdom: he therein portrays the middle classes and their functionaries as riddled with avarice, cruelty and vanity. Rouault's treatment of bourgeois dignitaries is as unrelievedly sombre as Bloy's; it has little of Daumier's mocking humor or Forain's stylish levity. The magnificent oil sketch, *Three Judges* (page 52) and a second oil sketch, *The Judges* (page 52) are relentlessly sardonic images (they have been dated here as c. 1907 on the stylistic evidence of a third sketch dated 1907 by the artist and very similar in technique). Rouault's judges are usually presented as single figures or as perverse Trinities—the two most common forms of figure composition in his work. Occasionally, however, he has turned to a more complicated grouping as in *The Court* (page 53) of c. 1909, with its figures emerging like sulphurous apparitions from a molten gloom.

Paintings: 1910-1915

Toward 1910 Rouault completed the *Pierrot* (page 54) in which the use of pastel in combination with oil provides a new brilliance of color. By comparison with many earlier works, the picture typifies the emphasis upon a meditated balance of forms which recurs with increasing frequency as Rouault's career progresses. But his Expressionist torment of spirit was by no means spent at this early date. In 1911 he painted the fine *Mr. X* (page 57), an image of almost hypnotic power, its muted color and rich texture in strong contrast to the thin handling and comparative elegance of the *Pierrot*. It is a painting upon which we have first-hand evidence of considerable interest. Some years ago the painter was asked whether the picture portrayed a definite person. He replied: "You are too inquisitive in asking if Mr. X exists and if he has posed for me. He has existed eternally; he is reborn when you think he is dead. It is to forget Mr. X, who kept haunting my brain although I had not yet created him pictorially, that from 1897 on I painted Crucifixions, Flagellations, occasionally some pathetic clowns, prostitutes, certain types of living deadwood and various different landscapes. In painting this sort of thing—not to stir up malice or to incite class against class—I had no spiteful intentions, no particular grudge. But what do I honestly know about it, and *who* knows himself?"[44]

1911 is the date usually given for two of Rouault's circular ceramics (page 58), executed for him by the ceramist, Metthey. The *Head of Christ* is clearly a liturgical work, recalling Bloy's description in *La Femme Pauvre* of a figure in a painting by the "apocalyptic" artist, Lazare Druide: "His bloodstained face reflects the outrages of all the world—a world enveloped in a mantle of universal grief."[45] It is indicative of the spiritual harmony between Rouault and Bloy that their versions of Christ should have corresponded so closely. "When Bloy speaks of Jesus Christ, he can see Him only as very sensual, sorrowful, pathetic, . . . gasping and bleeding."[46] The words could apply to nearly all of Rouault's heads of Christ, to the ceramic mentioned above and to the painted version of the same subject which he completed in 1913 (page 62).

As has happened consistently throughout Rouault's career until recent years, he shifts abruptly from close-up images of sharp psychological focus to an art of more deliberate architectural symmetry and a more inclusive viewpoint. Thus around the years 1911-1912 he completed with Metthey the large ceramic of bathers here reproduced (page 59). During these years he also painted several compositions in which the figures are sectionalized into broad patterns contained by heavy black contours which recall window leading and create an abstract counterpoint of design. The *Group of Rustics* (page 61) and *Woman and Children* (page 60) typify this tendency which continues with single figures such as the *Wrestler* (page 60) of c. 1913.

In the paintings just mentioned the satirical tradition is abandoned, and Rouault draws nearer those Cubists and Post-Cubists who readily sacrificed emotional content for a new synthesis of invented forms. And though it is difficult to reconcile Rouault's use of heavy outlines with Cézanne's statement, "The contour escapes me," the formalism of the *Group of Rustics* and other Rouaults of this period was probably inspired partially by Cézanne's figure compositions. There is evidence that Cézanne was still much on his mind. The print, *The Monk* (page 94), would seem to date from c. 1910 because of its close similarity to Rouault's ceramics in tone and surface; it is quite obviously related to Cézanne's *Portrait of a Monk* (Uncle Dominic) of 1865-1867. Once again it is necessary to insist on the unwavering

18

regard which Rouault has felt for the great Post-Impressionist. He has referred to Cézanne as "that seer of painting"[47]; he has always and often spoken of him in terms of unlimited admiration.

One of Rouault's masterworks, the *Three Judges* (color plate opposite page 62) dates from 1913. Here the satirical impact is overwhelming. The bulging, greedy central figure, the wolfish colleague at the left, the complacent judge at the right—these figures are defined with remarkable economy and strength of drawing. But it is color which carries the structural weight, color applied in closely related dark tones to create an atmospheric depth, evocative and eminently believable. Describing a comparable version of the same subject, James Johnson Sweeney has written: "In such a work as this by Rouault we find the complete antithesis of classicism: an urgent eccentric vitality, a brilliant vigor, a hard intense abstraction and Celtic unfriendliness—a contemporary parallel of that terrifying formal distortion whereby primitive man knew how to create a vision of the super-real."[48]

In 1913, too, Rouault completed the first of a group of small paintings and drawings in crayon and watercolor, probably for the most part intended as notebook sketches. They testify to a virtue with which he is not always credited—a subtle and penetrating sense of humor. The savage satire of *Mr. X* and the *Three Judges* is softened in these little pictures; the artist's mirth is less bitter, his enjoyment openly avowed. The group, as represented in the exhibition, begins with *The Shriveled Buccaneer* (cat. no. 37), continues with *The Cook* (page 63) and *The Circus Trainer* (page 64) and survives the disasters of the war years with *The Lovely Madam X* (page 63), *Portrait of a Man* (cat. no. 42) and *Man with Spectacles* (page 64). As a critic has written, "Rouault is not above painting in slang."[49] These small

paintings and drawings are extraordinarily skillful in characterization, being no less admirable in their way than some of his larger canvases. Their humor is amply reinforced by that of many of the fine prints which Rouault executed in the 1920s and 1930s. "Ferocity," Ernest Hello once pointed out, "knows how to laugh."[50]

1916-1917: Climactic Works of Rouault's Middle Career

A surprising amount of important art was produced during the course of the First World War. From 1916 to 1918, for example, Rouault completed five or six paintings which supply a climax to his middle career, just as half a dozen major works of 1905 and 1906 represent the apogee of his early manner.

The two periods, early and middle, show profound differences of approach. By 1916 Rouault's spiritual crisis of 1905-1906 has abated somewhat. The artist's grief is still unassuaged, but his emotion is muted and controlled by a mature dignity; to vicious protest has succeeded a resignation which surrenders nothing of pity but much of hate. And this change in spirit is reflected in his increased interest in painterly methods. Though he began at this time the prints for *Miserere et Guerre*, with their eloquent compassion for the horrors of war, his painting is calmer and more skillful, as though he found in it a refuge from the external world. The *Head* (page 66), it is true, is almost certainly a portrait of a German officer, as may be proved by comparing it with the print *With neither life nor joy* (page 99)—from the *Miserere et Guerre* series. But for the most part he turned to less temporal subjects in his oil paintings. It may have been difficult for him to despise the bourgeoisie while it fought for the nation's life and while corruption wore uniform wherever it existed. In any case, his paintings

Self Portrait with Cap. 1926. Lithograph, 9⅛ x 6¾". Buchholz Gallery, New York.

André Suarès. 1926. Lithograph, 9½ x 7". Collection Jean Goriany.

of 1916-1918 are of clowns and religious subjects rather than of prostitutes and judges, and are distinguished by a new dexterity in the medium of oil.

If we compare either of the two versions of the *Palace of Ubu Roi* (pages 66 and 67) with the *Two Prostitutes* of ten years before, it becomes obvious that Rouault's color has attained a new subtlety of control. The slashing, nervous overwriting and the massed shadows of the earlier period have disappeared. Indeed, in occasional works of the war years, modeling is achieved almost entirely through gradation of soft tone, and line is merely accentual in function. The color is no longer handled as an atmospheric wash of dark and limited range, but is built up through repeated applications which give it a luminous quality. The tones are melded rather than contrasted, as they were ten years

before. The key is more brilliant and by 1917 included rose, bright yellow and pink in addition to the red, green, blue, white, brown, chrome and black of his earlier career.

Perhaps it would be an exaggeration to speak of a new objectivity in so persistently subjective an artist. Nevertheless there are signs at this period that the artist's emotion occasionally surfaced, however briefly. There is, for example, the *Portrait of Henri Lebasque* (page 65). The picture was painted when Lebasque was ill. His pallor and the strained expression of his face inspired Rouault to paint of his friend one of his few portraits in which emphasis is upon realism of characterization. If we compare this portrait with an obsessional, "abstract" image like *Mr. X*, the change in approach becomes clear. The *Portrait of Lebasque* is not a synthesis of recurrent images but an actual portrait, dominated by the appearance of its subject and carrying the unmistakable mark of a close sympathy between painter and sitter. Such realism is rare and refreshing in Rouault's painting, though among his prints are some of the most sensitive portraits in 20th century art (pages 13 and 20). They are mostly of artists and writers whom Rouault has known intimately; all are of men whose work he has deeply admired.

Four of the most ambitious paintings of Rouault's middle career, all of them in American collections, are: the *Three Clowns* (page 69); *Clownerie* (page 70); *The Old Clown* (page 68); and the *Crucifixion* (page 71). A reproduction of one of the four in an early state is dated 1913, and this suggests that all four occupied the artist for several years. The brightest in color is *Clownerie*, its glowing yellows, reds, greens and blues amazingly intense beneath its chalky surface. This painting's off-center pyramidal composition is repeated in the *Three Clowns*, but the latter picture is more carefully arranged through a counterplay of squared and rounded subdivisions of the figures. By contrast, the asymmetrical unity of *Clownerie* depends in part upon a strange psychological rapport between the two figures, as though inspired by an actual incident observed by the painter. The smaller of the two figures, like the image of Ubu's palace, recurs frequently in Rouault's work, in other paintings and in prints for *Les Réincarnations du Père Ubu*.

In *The Old Clown* Rouault painted what may well be the outstanding work of his middle career. Unlike the *Portrait of Henri Lebasque*, the image is a generalized one of melancholy to which realism and individual characterization contribute little. It is an image whose plasticity, emotional force and magnificent color rank it high in modern art as a whole. Despite the seeming casualness of the background areas, the painting is also one of the most finished of Rouault's oils. The control of underpainting, the manner in which successive layers of pigment are allowed to break through to the surface or are coated over—is extremely sure and effective. But Rouault, who here reveals himself a master of "finish" in the unconventional sense of the word, deliberately left his *Crucifixion* of c. 1918 in an unfinished state, knowing that its values could be carried no further without sacrificing vigor for polish—an exchange he has seldom in his long career shown an inclination to make.

The Postwar Period

Professor Venturi in his recent monograph on Rouault states on the artist's authority that Rouault produced only a few paintings during the postwar decade, further that the painter does not recall having begun a new canvas after 1916, though he has reworked and often transformed entirely paintings already in his studio by that date. There are, however, several fine pastels from this period, among them *Head of a Woman* (page 73) and *Grotesque* (page 73); there are oils such as the *Three Judges* (cat. no. 55) and the major work, *Circus Trio* (page 72) which were probably well advanced by the end of the war. But for the most part during the years 1918-1928 Rouault was occupied with printmaking, due to the influence and demands of the bibliophile, Ambroise Vollard, who had become his exclusive dealer around 1916.

The loss of a decade of activity in easel painting is a serious one, though perhaps compensated for by the prints which have earned Rouault his position as one of the leading contemporary masters of the graphic arts. Since his years as a printmaker have strongly affected his more recent painting, his major print series will be discussed here briefly, to be followed by a description of his paintings since 1928.

21

The Prints for Miserere et Guerre

For nine long years—from 1916 to 1918 and again from 1920 to 1927—Rouault worked with fantastic devotion to satisfy the most strenuous demand made on any living artist by that master of exaction, Ambroise Vollard. The project was for 100 huge etchings to illustrate the text for *Miserere et Guerre* (two separate books appear to have been planned) written by André Suarès, a close friend of both Vollard and Rouault. The books have never been published; indeed, Vollard knew for several years before his death that they never would be. But 57 of the etchings were issued officially, a few more have appeared in varying states, and the incomplete series represents a prodigious accomplishment in the graphic arts. For if Picasso, Matisse and other leading contemporary masters have produced an impressive quantity of prints, none of them has worked so continuously, so long and concentratedly, in any print medium. None, surely, could have flourished in the shifting atmosphere of recrimination, reconciliation, abuse, praise, venom and balm which enveloped Rouault and Vollard during these nine years. The prints for *Miserere et Guerre*, if first-hand accounts may be credited, represent a distillate of an unending nervous crisis between artist and publisher. The themes of the prints are eternal, they deal with conflict and woe of the most broadly applicable kind, yet some of their impetus may have sprung from a tumult of lesser emotion, unrelentingly sublimated, larger than rancor, but grown perhaps from the steady exasperation which sometimes acts as the seed of grandeur itself.

As has been pointed out in a previous Museum publication,[51] and as Mr. Schniewind here confirms in detail, the first stage in making the etchings for *Miserere et Guerre* consisted in transferring photographically the artist's studies in gouache or other media to the copper plates. Unfortunately, none of these studies is available for reproduction, but the same photographic process was used in preparing the plates for *Les Réincarnations du Père Ubu*, and gouaches and finished etchings for that publication may be compared (pages 105 and 106). Once photographed on the copper plates, the painter's preliminary images were altered and transformed through extremely unconventional use of conventional engraver's tools and chemicals. But it is the use of this photogravure process which probably accounts for the exceptionally close relationship between Rouault's etchings and his paintings. Whereas most contemporary artists have executed prints as a logical complement to their drawings in ink or pencil, Rouault has almost literally painted on copper; the tonal range of his black and white etchings is basically coloristic.

The prints for *Miserere et Guerre* are perhaps Rouault's greatest accomplishment in the graphic arts and, quite apart from their extraordinary technical richness, are remarkable for their power and clarity as icons. (They do not depend upon given sequence for interest, so that it is of minor consequence that they have not been published in book form.) A few of them reveal the painter's hatred for such vultures of war as the *Society Woman* (page 96) and the German officer in *With neither life nor joy* (page 99). But it is the figure of Christ which dominates the series, recumbent and mourned in *In the press, the grape was trampled* (page 97), youthful and martyred in *St. Veronica's Veil* (cat. no. 89), on the cross unheeded in *Love ye one another* (cat. no. 101) which recalls Grünewald in its almost Germanic realism. (Rouault has written a poem in praise of Grünewald.)

Christ's wartime antagonist is Death, implacably waiting in *This will be the last, Little Father* (page 100), and cruelly half-victorious in *The blind will long be led by the halt* (page 99). Man appears as a professional performer turned helpless spectator in *Who does not frown?* (page

102), or lying armed and despairing amid the industrial supply houses of war with which he has replaced the cathedrals of Rouault's beloved Middle Ages (page 97). The artist's simplification of theme in these magnificent prints calls to mind his words written in praise of Daumier: "grandiose subjects have nothing to do with the matter, but only the talents, the power and the love of whomever treats the subject."[52]

The Frapier Prints: "Pitreries," "Grotesques," "Plutocratie," "Saltimbanques" (variously called). Portraits.

From c. 1924 to 1927 Rouault executed a number of lithographs, chiefly circus figures, satirical subjects and portraits, which were issued in Paris by the publisher, E. Frapier, to whom the artist in a very recent article refers with bitter humor as "Frapie, the little 'estampeur' "[53]—a pun on *estampe* and the slang word for pilferer. The inference is that Rouault himself does not know how many prints he completed for Frapier and did not know at the time. (Eighteen of the prints are reproduced in the catalog of the Neumann Gallery's Munich exhibition of Rouault, 1930, but many more were issued.) Some of the lithographs were used as plates in three Frapier books: *Les Peintres-Lithographes de Manet à Matisse* (1925); *Maîtres et Petit-Maîtres d'Aujourd'hui* (1926); and *Souvenirs Intimes* (1926), with text by Rouault. Apparently the publisher planned to issue a series of albums of the lithographs, to be grouped according to general subject, but the Frapier catalog of 1926 announces only one set, "Pitreries," and the other prints were probably all issued singly. With several notable exceptions such as the *Acrobat* (page 103) and the *Prostitute* (cat. no. 123), the finest of the Frapier prints are portraits of men whom Rouault had known well and re-

vered—Gustave Moreau (page 13), J. K. Huysmans (cat. no. 132), Léon Bloy (page 13) and André Suarès (page 20). Too subjective an artist to become interested in portraiture for its own objective sake, the painter in these lithographs has recorded with rare acuteness the personalities of those few friends who had been an inseparable part of his inner life.

Petite Banlieue

In 1929 the Galerie Quatre Chemins in Paris issued 100 sets of six Rouault lithographs, entitled *Petite Banlieue;* two of the sets were hand colored by the artist. In these prints Rouault turned to the depiction of the shoddy, industrial suburbs which he loathes by comparison with the city and open country. The temper of his landscape art is usually grave and melancholy, suggesting Jacques Maritain's description of Léon Bloy's conception of nature—"Wild storms, dark nights, tears of bitter mysticism in a violent, passionate sky above an indomitable earth . . ."[54] But Rouault's landscapes, for all their traditional romanticism of mood, are unmistakably contemporary: the eloquent flat patterns of *Burial of Hope* (page 108) stem from the Post-Impressionist tradition of an Edvard Munch; the print's dramatic starkness is close in spirit to the graphic art of Rouault's German contemporaries in Expressionism.

Paysages Légendaires

Also in 1929, Rouault completed six lithographs and fifty drawings for a book of his own poems, *Paysages Légendaires*, issued by Editions Porteret, Paris. The book reveals an unexpected facet of the artist's psychology—a nostalgia for the elegant civilization of *Le roi soleil* at Versailles to which one would think him by nature wholly indifferent. In both poems and illustrations, the book alternates between the artist's usual troubled and compassionate vision and a longing for the gay splendor of Le Nôtre's gardens and soft lagoons. To his youthful nightmare of the *maisons closes*, he now opposes a daydream of *fêtes galantes*. From the image of Christ and the Fishermen, he turns abruptly to an evocation of the Embarcation for Cytheria (page 109)—

> "*Habit de cour et de gala*
> *il serait beau d'y voir encore*
> *Monsieur Watteau*
> *Venez dans mon bateau*
> *Monsieur Watteau*
> *suivons le fil de la rivière*
> *en rêverie légendaire*
> *loin des soucis arbitraires*"

But such escapist dreams furnish only temporary comfort for the artist, and the mood of religious fervor and brooding returns

> "*Ayant connaisance de tant de choses*
> *vaines et moroses*
> *j'ai tout oublié et perdu la mémoire ce soir*
> *—la triste histoire—*
> *revienne matin de printemps*
> *harmonie secrète me berçant*
> *la fée Mélancolie*
> *dira entre ses petites dents*
> *coupantes comme le diamant*
> *—Georget rêveur impénitent*
> *tu finiras sur l'échafaud—*
> *idéaliste tourmentant*"

Les Réincarnations du Père Ubu

On December 10, 1896, at the *Théâtre de l'Oeuvre* in Paris, one of the most celebrated evenings in the late 19th century French theatre took place—the presentation of Alfred Jarry's *Ubu Roi*, with music by Claude Terrasse and décor by Bonnard and Géruzier. Jarry had written the play at the incredible age of fifteen. It had originally been conceived for marionettes, and was so performed for the first time at the *Théâtre des Phynances* in 1888. But as revived in 1896, it was produced with living actors. Was Ambroise Vollard in the audience? In any case, the play became one of the passions of the publisher's life, and finally he wrote several sequels to it, among them *Les Réincarnations du Père Ubu*, which Rouault illustrated with 22 etchings and 104 wood-engravings, the latter

cut on wood by the master engraver, Georges Aubert.

As early as 1913, if we may accept one of the two dates which appear on a gouache later used as the basis for a print (page 106), Rouault, too, had become an enthusiast for *Ubu Roi*, and by 1918 a good number of his gouache studies for *Les Réincarnations du Père Ubu* were completed. In 1916 he began work on the etchings themselves, and in that same year painted the two oil versions of the palace of Ubu which have already been mentioned. The strange phallic mosque of the palace facade, Byzantine in spirit, was to become for him a dominant architectural image. It recurs in several of his landscapes (pages 66 and 67), it appears in his ballet setting for "Prodigal Son" (page 75), it reappears in prints of the *Passion* series (page 112). Rouault's vision of the palace is an abstract one, and it is interesting to note that this accords with Jarry's own intention. The palace is located at Warsaw in the play, *Ubu Roi*, but Jarry had made clear that none of the stage properties should suggest specific time or place. Thus his instructions to the impresario of the *Théâtre de l'Oeuvre* call for "Costumes with as little local or chronological color as possible (which will better render the idea of an eternal theme), modern preferred, since the satire is modern; and sordid because the drama will thereby seem more miserable and horrific."[55] Rouault's own conception of the palace is widely symbolic: the mosque stands as the castle of the fantastic Ubu, king of Poland; it reappears in Jerusalem as backdrop to the sad travail of Christ.

Jarry himself had made several drawings of his central character, Ubu, and had designed the marionettes originally used at the *Théâtre des Phynances*. He had imagined Ubu as a pudgy, pontifical figure, with heavy jowls and large, bridgeless nose jutting from a steep forehead. (His marionette of Ubu is reproduced in

24

Soirées de Paris for May 15, 1914, page 292.)
Rouault's image of Ubu is comparable, though
more scathing and more insistent on the su-
preme effrontery of Ubu's mentality which
Jarry's prose, rather than his drawings, developed. The mordant humor of Jarry's master-
piece, as continued in Vollard's text, colors
nearly all of Rouault's fine and surprisingly
literal illustrations for *Les Réincarnations du
Père Ubu*. The artist's scorn bites deep in his
print of two lovers, snarling and bestial (cat.
no. 142) and in his depiction of Ubu's intimates
(page 104). In his dragon (page 107) he created
one of the most original and penetrating fan-
tasies in modern graphic art—an hallucinatory
monster, but real as a noon sweat of fear.

The Recent Color Plates

During the 1930s Rouault completed a number
of color etchings for three Vollard publications:
Le Cirque, with text by Suarès (as yet unpublished); *Le Cirque de l'Etoile Filante* (1938),
with text by the artist; and *Passion* (1939),
with text by Suarès. The prints for all three
publications have been avidly collected, and
have done much in this country to further
Rouault's fame. Nevertheless, a majority of
these prints suffer by comparison with the
painter's superb black and white etchings and
make his words on Daumier seem appropriate
to his own prints: "What a painter he is, with
his rare quality of blacks and whites . . ."[56] The
color etchings of the 1930s are seldom as con-
vincing or inspired as the technically less ambitious color prints of 1910, such as the *Clown
with Monkey* (page 94), with its curious resemblance to finger painting on a porcelain surface, or the vigorous lithograph, *The Horseman*
(page 93). The plates for Vollard's three recent
books often seem static, hard and lacking in
inner life, very probably for the technical reasons which Mr. Schniewind explains. Rouault's
nervous force and passion are missing in many
of these plates to some degree, as though fidelity
of spirit had been lost in the search for ac-
curacy of tone, as though the artist's unorthodox but eloquent technique in black and white
etching—"they give me a copper plate, and I
just dig into it"[57]—had been overly complicated
by the need for continuous technical assistance
in the multiplate process of color etching.

Recent Paintings: 1929-1939

When Rouault began again to paint steadily,
around 1929, his art almost immediately reflected a widening of inspirational source. Indeed, the words of a critic on Moreau might
safely be applied to that master's favorite
pupil: "His language has everything—Greek,
Byzantine, Persian, perhaps even Chinese."[58]
During the 1920s, Rouault had read widely and
himself become a writer of both prose and
poetry, uneven in quality, frequently obscu-
rantist or uneasily primitive, but sometimes
illumined by the same force and passion which
give his art its distinction. It seems likely, too,
that his literary studies were combined with
more extensive research into the art of the past
than he had undertaken before (and here
Vollard's influence must have counted strongly). His paintings of 1929-1939 indicate an
appreciation of Byzantine enamels, Roman
mosaics and Coptic tapestries. But surely the
paramount influence on his recent career has
been his own activity as a printmaker; it is an
influence felt both in the slight broadening of
his iconographical range and in a new technical
fluency.

As represented in the present exhibition, his
recent painting begins with the fine self portrait
(page 74), said, oddly enough, to have been
posed for by the artist's son. The same year,
1929, he completed a number of gouache heads
which are variable in quality, though occasionally both ambitious and successful (page 76).
Perhaps in the first flush of liberation from the

long years of printmaking, he worked too quickly. In any case his gouache heads of 1929 and 1930 are often rather superficial by comparison with his pre-war paintings, as though he relied upon an automatic earmark of style. For Rouault's art is so aggressively personal that he must sometimes slap its face; he appears to have done so in the *Christ in Profile* (page 82) in which the yellow area of the neck is deliberately allowed to dominate the stylistic content of the painting as a whole.

The humor of *Man with Derby* (cat. no. 63) is carried over from a print of the same subject, and his landscape prints, executed in so varied a technique, contributed importantly to his painted landscapes of 1929 and 1930. *At Gentilly* (page 78), for example, is close in technique and spirit to prints from the *Miserere* and *Petite Banlieue* series, though not unrelated to the wash drawings which Gustave Moreau did in Italy in the late 1850s. It stands as one of his most powerful landscapes, with its factory chimneys like three broken crosses, its desolate chiaroscuro of ruined land, its unholy violence of industrial light exploding the sky. But beyond the ravaged suburbs, Rouault could still discover an untrammeled nature, as in the *Afterglow, Galilee* (page 81) which foretells his more recent landscapes in splendor of color.

Gradually, as the tension of completing his major print series relaxed, Rouault began again to explore the seductive qualities of oil pigment. His *Head of Pierrot* (cat. no. 72), *Head of a Clown* (page 85) and *Woman's Head* (page 84) approach the ideal of art for its own sake which his figure pieces of 1905 and 1906 had so strenuously repudiated. His acceptance of this ideal, in the serenity of older age, is indicated by the decorative device of the painted frame within the picture which he has used in recent works (pages 88 and 89).

Four major paintings of the mid-1930s are the *Christ Mocked by Soldiers* (color plate opposite page 82), *The Last Romantic* (page 87), *The Old King* (color frontispiece) and *Dwarf* (page 86). A comparison between *Christ Mocked* and such a painting as the *Three Clowns* of 1917 reveals the full complication of Rouault's recent palette. Whereas in the latter picture the tonal areas were fairly broad and pure, the *Christ Mocked* is a synthesis of relatively local touches, sometimes applied to the surface but more often achieved by letting the endless undercoats come through under varied and tight control. If the word had not become so specialized in meaning, the technique of *Christ Mocked* might be described as an encrusted Impressionism; certainly its vibrancy is Impressionist in contrast to the still power of the *Three Clowns*.

The Old King is known to have been begun in 1916, though not completed until 1936, and it seems likely that *The Last Romantic* was also worked on over a long period of years. Both paintings are so heavily painted as to justify a critic's description of certain Rouaults as "rotten with color,"[59] and in their relief modeling they belong to the tradition of such early Cézannes as the *Washing of a Corpse* of 1867-1869. Both are icons of exceptional strength and conviction, angular in contour, Gothic, hard, implacable, but glowing with an inner illumination as though they, like Rouault's beloved stained glass, let through a warming light. With them must be grouped the fine *Dwarf*: all three paintings have a grandeur which comes in large part from their condensation, their obsessional force as images seen repeatedly in the artist's dreams, looming forward and desperately near from the surrounding dark. There is supplementary evidence that the subject of *The Last Romantic* had a special hold on the artist in that he intended the picture as a satirical self portrait. He has often referred ironically to a critic's description of him as "the last romantic," and once wrote: "However great a talent is needed to produce

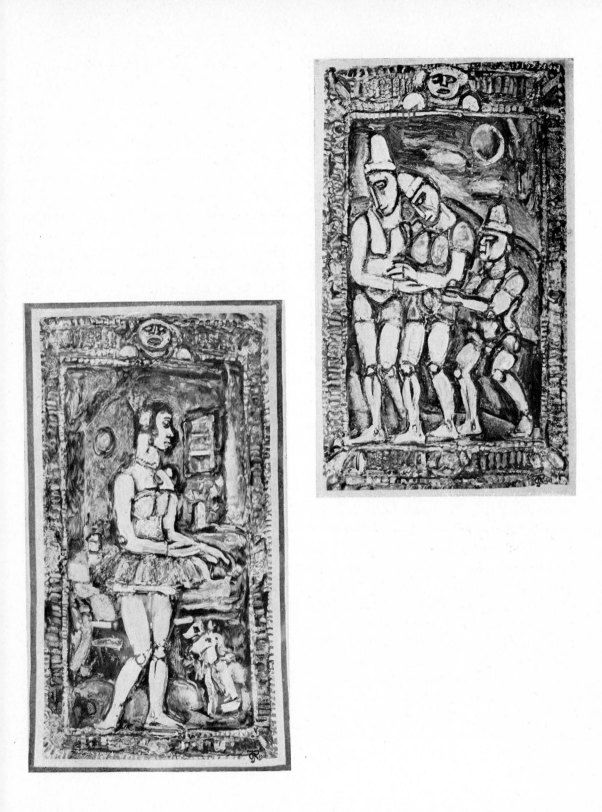

Left: *The Dancer. 1931. Wool tapestry, 89¾ x 50½″. Collection Mme. Marie Cuttoli.*

Right: *Wounded Clown. 1931. Wool tapestry, 76⅝ x 46⅛″. Collection Mme. Marie Cuttoli.*

St. Veronica's Veil. 1932. Wool tapestry, 32½ x 28½". Collection Mme. Marie Cuttoli.

David's *Leonidas at Thermopylae*, for example, many more modest works (I am thinking of the unobtrusive Chardins, of the *Christ at Emmaus* by Rembrandt . . . of Poussin's *Diogenes*) go far more directly to my heart—I am not afraid of employing this rather old-fashioned word, having been called 'the last of the Romantics.'"[60]

The tormented vision exemplified by these three pictures is relaxed in the *Pierrot with a Rose* (page 88) which, unlike the three, was probably completely painted in the late 1930s.

In this and other recent pictures Rouault has turned to a new lyricism of color which reaches perhaps its purest form in still life subjects (page 89). The rage of his early period (1903-1906) has abated almost entirely; the melancholy of his middle years (1915-1918) has lifted so that even a relatively tragic subject like *The Wounded Clown* (page 92) is treated fairly dispassionately, and depends for its impact upon more traditional esthetic qualities which survive to an exceptional degree the picture's translation into tapestry (page 27). Considering his still lifes and figure pieces of 1939, it seems possible that Rouault predicted wrongly when, in praising Renoir for very opposite attainments, he described himself as "prisoner of shadows until my death."[61]

"Glory to you," he adds in speaking of Renoir, "for often having been drunk with color when so many others sought only a mediocre success and withered away."[62] He himself, just before the present war, showed signs of that resurgence of spirit, expressed through color, which carried Renoir into his strong late period. We know now, and thankfully, that Rouault is well and living in the country in France. A statement by him, very recently reported here, confirms the serene direction his art is taking: "I spent my life painting twilights. I ought to have the right now to paint the dawn."[63]

JAMES THRALL SOBY

THE TECHNIQUE OF GEORGES ROUAULT'S PRINTS

The reconstruction of Rouault's various graphic techniques is full of interesting and rather puzzling problems. Without having all of the available material at hand, such as trial proofs, impressions from individual color plates and so on, a technical analysis of Rouault's prints becomes guess work to a very great extent. Nevertheless the following observations may help somewhat to clarify the situation, if only to establish what is not clear about his methods. Rouault's strong and unconventional personality has made him an unorthodox printmaker from the first. He rarely, if ever, uses a given medium in the usual way, but immediately begins to experiment with it, achieving completely different results from any other printmaker.

In lithography his methods on the whole deviate least from the usual ones. The almost exclusive use of lithographic wash or *tusch* in connection with scraping out the lights and highlights is not found very often and no one, certainly, has made such masterly use of all of its possibilities. The natural softness of the lithographic wash is brought to further refinements through Rouault's careful selection of the paper which he uses for printing. The finest impressions are either pulled on a firm, moderately thin and very smooth Chinese paper (as in the *Self Portrait without a Cap*, existing in impressions in color or in black only) which has a slightly gray tone or on a heavy cream-colored or even tan Japanese paper. In a few cases Rouault has chosen a soft paper with a rough surface texture (from the Gaspard Maillol mill), but they are not the most successful of his experiments.

In all probability Rouault has always worked directly on the stone. I can find no evidence of the use of the transfer methods seen in so many other modern lithographs (Cézanne, Matisse, Derain, Bonnard, etc.). His approach to the lithograph is very much that of a water-colorist or of some one working with a broad wash of a single color.

The methods he uses in making his black and white and his colored etchings are as complicated and indirect as his lithographs seem to be comparatively simple and direct. I feel that we know only partly how they are made and that only a first-hand statement from the artist and from his printer will really clarify the whole procedure. Nevertheless the following facts seem to me to be quite certain:

In the large unpublished plates for *Miserere et Guerre* and in the small plates for *Les Réincarnations du Père Ubu*, all of which are printed in only one color, Rouault has combined numerous hand processes together with a photomechanical process. Through the photomechanical process he establishes his working base—his underpaint, so to speak, on the metal plate. This "base" disappears almost entirely under the extensive handwork to which he subjects the plate.

After Vollard's death a trial proof of the large plate *Tenderness* was found which clearly revealed the first step in the making of these etchings (page 30). This proof, which is now owned by the Art Institute of Chicago, is nothing other than a photomechanical reproduction of a gouache or oil painting. The reproduction has been photoengraved onto the metal plate, which is probably copper. The impression from the plate in this state shows the brush strokes of the original and the three-dimensionality of

Miserere et Guerre: *Tenderness, 1922. 22¾ x 16¼". The Art Institute of Chicago.* Left: *Impression from photogravure plate before handwork was applied.* Right: *After etching and aquatint were applied.*

the paint (see enlarged detail). There are no traces of any handwork on the plate. I have also had opportunity to verify this first stage of Rouault's method when I was once shown some of the original gouaches for *Le Père Ubu.* Undoubtedly they, too, had been transferred photographically (photoengraved) onto the metal plate before Rouault began to work on it.* The plates, thus prepared, were then taken in hand by Rouault who proceeded to rework the entire surface of the plate by manual processes. These consist mainly of extensive application of aquatint, the use of the roulette in

small sections, free application of drypoint lines, with heavy burr, direct biting of the plate with acid which is applied with a brush, and scraping away parts of the preliminary photoengraved work. Thus almost nothing seems to remain of the photoengraving but, on close study, it will be found that Rouault has carefully blended the photographic and the manual parts of the work, leaving the photoengraved structure wherever he can achieve effects through it which are unobtainable by hand (the three-dimensional qualities of the painting's impasto, for instance). The indirectness of this method—preparation of the plate by reproducing on it a preliminary oil or gouache sketch through photomechanical means—is, at first, somewhat puzzling. But when the results are studied we can readily

* I have not attempted to explain, here, the technical process involved in the photomechanical preparation of the metal plate. The method is fairly complicated and has no direct bearing on the manual part of Rouault's work. The preparatory reproduction of the gouache on the plate is done, of course, by some commercial firm.

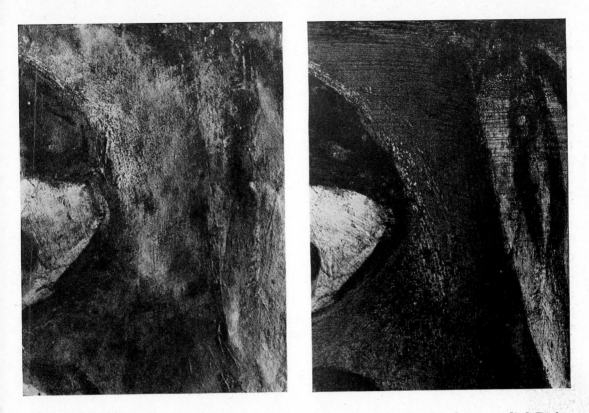

Detail of *Tenderness*. Left: *Impression from photogravure plate before handwork was applied.* Right: *After etching and aquatint was applied.*

understand that the regular manual methods alone would have failed to obtain them. Rouault has indeed brought new life into the time-worn methods of traditional etching. Through his method he succeeds in transforming into black and white the entire spirit of the preliminary painting and, though he has completely covered and transformed the quality of the lines and surfaces of the painting, he has preserved the rhythm of the brush strokes and its basic design.

The mixture of photomechanical and hand processes is not new in printmaking though their combined use never resulted, hitherto, in anything but a saving of time and effort on the artist's part. Félicien Rops used to retouch heliogravures of drawings extensively with drypoint and etching, but these prints are far from possessing the clarity and richness of tone of Rouault's work and they have always a certain mechanical appearance.

The Color Aquatints

There has been much speculation over the technique of Rouault's illustrations in color for *La Passion, Le Cirque* and *Le Cirque de l'Etoile Filante*. The many colors which were used for the printing of these plates make positive analysis of the technique a very difficult task indeed. The numerous layers of printed color, one over the other, fill up the surface so thoroughly that the texture of the individual color is lost and with it some of the best clues for detecting the actual methods which were involved. The colors were achieved by printing from a number of individual color plates. Seven or even more plates seem to have been used. The predominant technique in each plate appears to be aquatint. Probably here, too, a preparatory photomechanical reproduction was made, possibly only on the black outline plate. I have been able to detect remnants of the preliminary painting's impasto in the black portions only. It would also seem quite unnecessary to repeat the preparatory photomechanical preparation on each color plate. The color plates seem to be pure aquatint. Contrary to previous belief, I do not think that part of the colors were printed from lithographic stones. The basic aquatint texture can be detected throughout. The coarseness of this grain is varied in order to obtain various textures. This granular structure is supplemented with roulette and with a toothed instrument which was probably similar to a mezzotint rocker. In some spots the etching ground shows a kind of "craquelure" which has been bitten into the plate. Drypoint lines with abundant burr have been used in the various color plates as well as in the black key plate.

The actual printing of these plates must have been done in a way similar to the methods used in 18th century color-printing. Each plate is perforated with two small holes which are located about half an inch from the top and the bottom, toward the center of the plate. These holes are located at exactly the same spot on each set of plates. Two pins are driven into the table of the printing press so that they can be fitted into the holes of the plate. The pins are pointed at the top and only slightly longer than the thickness of the plate. These pins make slight holes in the paper when the print is pulled. The pin marks help to fit the paper over the next plate which is held in its exact place by the two pins. Furthermore in changing plates the sheet is held firmly in place. The holes in the plates are made at some concealed spot on the plate, since they leave slight marks —the register marks. In some of the experimental plates for the *Cirque de l'Etoile Filante* set, where the registration is not quite perfect, the register marks are on the sides of the plates. These marks can be seen as fine holes when holding the sheet against the light.

In book illustration the French have used stencils (pochoirs) extensively in coloring plates, but I do not believe that they have been used in Rouault's prints. In rare instances very slight high lights seem to have been added, but it appears from their irregularity that these were applied free hand and not with stencils. On a few plates the reds show a special brilliance. This was probably achieved through touching up the printed surface either with shellac, gum arabic or white of egg, an old trick used extensively by the lithograph colorists of Daumier's time.

The printing of these particular colored sets, which undoubtedly was not done by Rouault himself but by a very skilled professional printer, represents a high degree of technical achievement. But the prints always appear to have a certain mechanical quality about them. This may be due to the fact that the color scheme, which is particularly lavish, is somewhat overdone. The original freshness of the concept is stiffened through the numerous mechanical steps which become necessary to obtain the highly complicated final result.

CARL O. SCHNIEWIND

The Ordeal of Samson. 1893. Oil on canvas, 57¾ x 44⅞″. Collection Mr. and Mrs. Maurice Sterne.

The Quarry. 1897. Gouache and pastel, 32½ x 41″. Collection Mme. Henry Simon.

Left: *Costumed Men. 1906 (?). Watercolor, 6⅞ x 4½". Collection Leonard C. Hanna, Jr.*

Right: *Head of Young Girl. 1904. Oil and gouache, 9⅞ x 7⅝". Collection Mr. and Mrs. Carl O. Schniewind.*

Babel. 1905–06 (?). Oil, 23 x 31½". Collection Miss Mary Rumsey.

The Couple. 1905. Galerie Kaganovitch, Paris. Not in the exhibition.

Left: *Woman with Red Stockings. 1905 (?). Gouache, 11⅞ x 7½". Collection Albert Sarraut.*

Right: *Woman with a Mirror. 1905. Gouache, 9⅞ x 8¼". Collection Dr. Girardin.*

Nude Torso. c. 1906. Gouache, 15⅜ x 12¾". The Art Institute of Chicago.

Prostitutes. 1906. Collection M. Witzinger, Basel. Not in the exhibition.

The Sirens. 1906. Gouache, 28 x 22¼". Collection R. Sturgis Ingersoll.

Clown with Theatre Box. 1906. Gouache and watercolor, 37¾ x 25¾".
Collection Mme. Henry Simon.

Circus Woman. 1906. Pastel and gouache, 27 x 20″. Private collection.

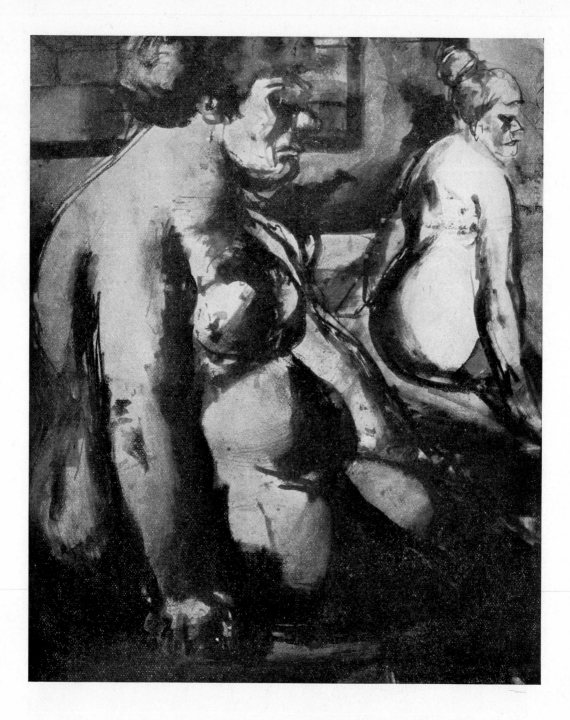

Two Prostitutes. 1906. Watercolor, 26½ x 24¼". Collection Dr. and Mrs. Harry Bakwin.

Woman at a Table. 1906. Watercolor,
12½ x 9¼". The Museum of Modern
Art, acquired through the Lillie P. Bliss
Bequest.

Nude. 1905. Watercolor,] 18 x 14½".
Private collection.

Head of a Clown. c. 1907. Oil on paper, 15½ x 12¼". Private collection.

Clown. c. 1907–08. Oil on paper, 23⅝ x 18½". The Dumbarton Oaks Research Library and Collection, Harvard University (Robert Woods Bliss Collection).

Odalisque. 1907. Collection Max Bangerter, Paris. Not in the exhibition.

Bathers. 1908. Watercolor, 18 x 23½". Collection Dr. and Mrs. MacKinley Helm.

Bathers. 1908–10. Oil on composition board, 19 x 22". Collection Mme. Carlos Martins.

Red-Haired Woman. 1908. Gouache and watercolor, 27 x 19¼". Collection Lt. and Mrs. Lee A. Ault.

Nude. 1909. Gouache and oil, 39⅞ x 25½″. Private collection.

The Judges. c. 1907. Oil on paper, 24¾ x 22¼″. The Portland Art Museum.

Three Judges. c. 1907. Oil on paper, 14 x 22″. Collection Mr. and Mrs. Samuel A. Marx.

The Court. c. 1909. Oil on panel, 30¼ x 42⅛". Collection Max Bangerter.

Pierrot. 1910. Oil and pastel on paper, 33¼ x 19¼". Collection Lt. and Mrs. Joseph Pulitzer, Jr.

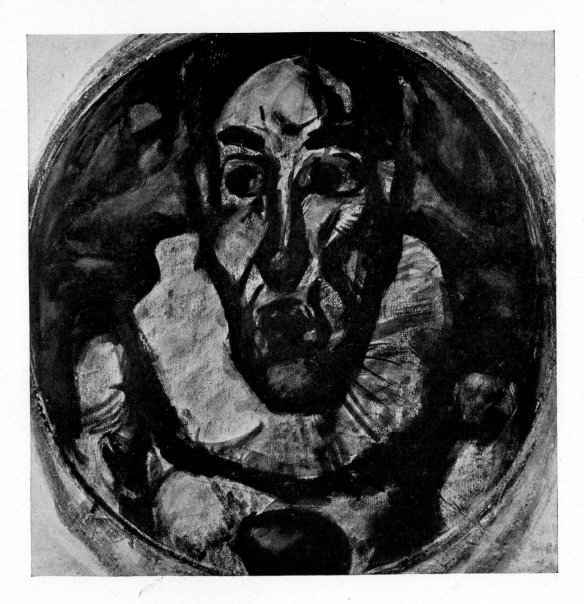

Head of a Clown. c. 1910. Gouache, 20 x 20″. Collection Dr. F. H. Hirschland.

Left: *Head of a Worker. 1911. Oil on paper, 15½ x 11¼″. Collection Mr. and Mrs. Ralph F. Colin.*

Right: *Make-Up, Cirque Forain. 1911. Oil and gouache, 14 x 11″. Collection Mme. Carlos Martins.*

56

Mr. X. 1911. Oil on paper, 29½ x 21½". Albright Art Gallery, Buffalo.

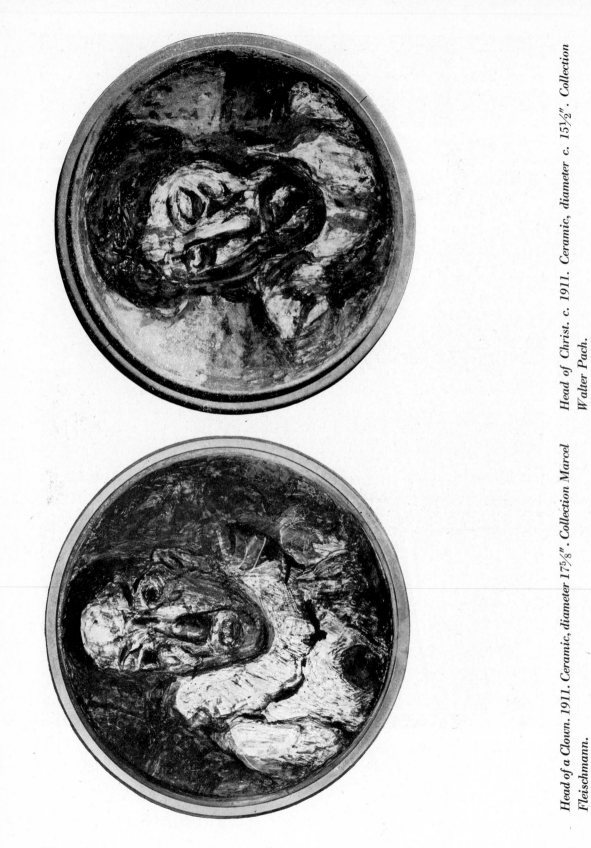

Head of a Clown. 1911. Ceramic, diameter 17⅝". Colléction Marcel Fleischmann.

Head of Christ. c. 1911. Ceramic, diameter c. 15½". Collection Walter Pach.

Bathers. 1910–12 (?). Ceramic. Not in the exhibition.

Left: *Wrestler. c. 1913. Gouache, 12 x 8″. Pierre Matisse Gallery.*

Right: *Woman and Children. 1912. Gouache on cardboard, 12½ x 8⅝″. Collection Marcel Fleischmann.*

Group of Rustics. 1911. Gouache and pastel, 28 x 25". Pierre Matisse Gallery.

Head of Christ. 1913. Oil on porcelain, 18¼ x 14¼". Collection Miss Helen L. Resor.

Three Judges. 1913. Oil on canvas, 28⅜ x 40¼". Collection Mr. and Mrs. Sam A. Lewisohn.

Left: *The Cook. 1914. Gouache on paper, 14 x 9¾". Collection Mr. and Mrs. Sam A. Lewisohn.*

Right: *The Lovely Madam X. 1915. Gouache on paper, 13¾ x 9⅜". Collection Mr. and Mrs. Sam A. Lewisohn.*

Left: *Man with Spectacles. 1917. Watercolor, 11¾ x 6½". The Museum of Modern Art, gift of Mrs. John D. Rockefeller, Jr.*

Right: *The Circus Trainer. 1915. Gouache, watercolor and crayon, 15½ x 10⅜". Perls Galleries.*

Portrait of Henri Lebasque. 1917. Oil on canvas, 36¼ x 28⅞". The Museum of Modern Art, Purchase Fund.

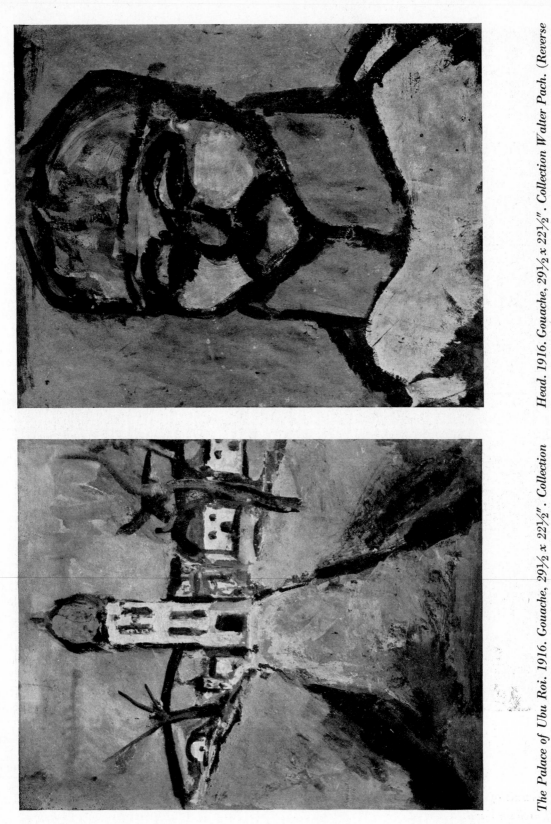

The Palace of Ubu Roi. 1916. Gouache, 29½ x 22½". Collection Walter Pach.

Head. 1916. Gouache, 29½ x 22½". Collection Walter Pach. (Reverse side of picture at left.)

The Palace of Ubu Roi. 1916. Gouache, 29 x 41½". Collection Mr. and Mrs. Ralph M. Coe.

The Old Clown. 1917. Oil, 44¼ x 29⅜″. Collection Edward G. Robinson, Hollywood. Not in the exhibition.

Three Clowns. 1917. Oil on canvas, 41½ x 29½". Collection Lt. and Mrs. Joseph Pulitzer, Jr.

Clownerie. c. 1917. Oil on canvas, 40½ x 28½″. Collection Lt. Wright Ludington.

Crucifixion. c. 1918. Oil on canvas, 41¼ x 29⅝". Collection Lt. Henry P. McIlhenny, U.S.N.R.

Circus Trio. c. 1924. Oil on paper, 30 x 42". The Phillips Memorial Gallery.

Head of a Woman. 1927. Pastel, 11 x 9".
Collection Werner Feuz.

Grotesque. 1927. Pastel, 12½ x 9". Collection
Werner Feuz.

73

Self Portrait. 1929. Gouache, 20¼ x 14¼". Collection Lt. and Mrs. Lee A. Ault.

74

Design for décor for Ballet: The Prodigal Son. *1929. Watercolor, 20¼ x 28¾".*
The Wadsworth Atheneum, Hartford.

Design for décor for Ballet: The Prodigal Son. *1929. Watercolor, 20 x 28¼". The*
Wadsworth Atheneum, Hartford.

Figure. 1929. Oil, gouache and pastel on cardboard, 22 x 16¼". Collection Bernard J. Reis.

Clown. 1930. Oil, 11 x 8½". Collection Miss Helen L. Resor.

At Gentilly. 1929. Gouache and watercolor, 14 x 20″. Collection Elmer Rice.

Tragic Face. 1930. Oil, 22 x 19¾″. Collection Mr. and Mrs. Sam A. Lewisohn.

The Funeral. 1930. Gouache and pastel, 11 x 19⅜". The Museum of Modern Art, given anonymously.

Face to Face. c. 1930. Oil and gouache on paper, 13¼ x 12¾". Collection Mr. and Mrs. R. Kirk Askew, Jr.

Afterglow, Galilee. c. 1930. Oil on canvas, 19⅝ x 25½". The Phillips Memorial Gallery.

Christ in Profile. 1930 (?). Oil on canvas, 28¾ x 23¾". Collection Miss Mary E. Johnston.

Christ Mocked by Soldiers. 1932. Oil on canvas, 36¼ x 28½". The Museum of Modern Art, given anonymously.

Polichinelle. c. 1930. Oil on paper, 28½ x 20". Collection Mr. and Mrs. Walter C. Arensberg.

Woman's Head. c. 1936. Oil on composition board, 31⅛ x 25¼". Collection Marcel Fleischmann.

Head of a Clown. c. 1936. Oil on canvas, 9¾ x 7½". Collection Mr. and Mrs. Vladimir Golschmann.

Dwarf. c. 1936. Oil on canvas, 27⅛ x 19¾". Bignou Gallery.

The Last Romantic. c. 1937. Oil on wood, 26⅞ x 19¾". Collection Dr. and Mrs. Harry Bakwin.

Pierrot with a Rose. c. 1936. Oil on canvas, 36¾ x 24½". Collection Mr. and Mrs. Samuel S. White, III.

Bouquet. c. 1938. Oil, 35 x 23¾". Collection Mr. and Mrs. Ralph F. Colin.

Turbaned Woman. 1939. Oil on paper, 21¼ x 16″. Collection Lionello Venturi.

Nocturne. 1939. Oil, 28 x 39″. Collection Miss Mary E. Johnston.

Landscape. 1939. Oil on canvas, 16¼ x 22″. Collection Lionello Venturi.

The Wounded Clown. 1939. Oil, 71 x 46". Private collection.

The Horseman (Le Conducteur de Chevaux). 1910. Color lithograph, 13⅛ x 17½". The Brooklyn Museum.

Left: *The Monk. 1910(?). Lithograph, 11⅞ x 8½". Buchholz Gallery.*

Right: *Clown with Monkey. 1910. Monotype, 24¼ x 15". Collection Mr. and Mrs. Sam A. Lewisohn.*

Left: *The Hideous Woman. 1918. Etching, 10¼ x 6⅝". Collection Jean Goriany.*

Right: *The Hideous Woman. 1919. Etching with aquatint, 12⅛ x 7¾". Collection Jean Goriany.*

95

Left: Miserere et Guerre: *Society Woman. 1922. Etching, 22½ x 16¼". The Museum of Modern Art, Extended Loan.*

Right: Miserere et Guerre: *Two Grotesques. 1922. Etching, 22⅜ x 16¼". Collection Jean Goriany.*

Top: Miserere et Guerre: *Man is a wolf to man.* 1927. Etching, *16⅝ x 23½″*. *The Museum of Modern Art, Extended Loan.*

Bottom: Miserere et Guerre: *In the press, the grape was trampled.* 1922. Etching, *15½ x 19″*. *The Museum of Modern Art, Extended Loan.*

Miserere et Guerre: *The Deposition. 1926. Etching, 23 x 16½". Collection Miss Ann C. Resor.*

Left: Miserere et Guerre: *With neither life nor joy. 1926. Etching, 23 x 16⅝". The Museum of Modern Art, Extended Loan.*

Right: Miserere et Guerre: *The Blind will long be led by the halt. 1920. Etching, 23⅛ x 17⅛". The Museum of Modern Art, Extended Loan.*

Miserere et Guerre: *This will be the last, Little Father. 1927. Etching, 23⅛ x 16⅞".*
The Museum of Modern Art, Extended Loan.

100

Miserere et Guerre: *Louis XI (Ambroise Vollard?). 1926(?). Etching, 22¾ x 16⅜".*
Collection Jean Goriany.

Miserere et Guerre: *Who does not frown? 1923. Etching, 22¼ x 16⅞". The Museum of Modern Art, Extended Loan.*

Left: *The Strong Man* (E. Frapier). *Lithograph, 13⅛ x 8⅞". The Brooklyn Museum.*

Right: *Acrobat* (E. Frapier). *c.1925. Lithograph, 12½ x 9". The Museum of Modern Art, given anonymously.*

Left: Les Réincarnations du Père Ubu. *1928. Etching, 10⅝ x 7⅜". The Museum of Modern Art, Extended Loan.*

Right: Les Réincarnations du Père Ubu. *1928. Etching, 11⅝ x 7⅜". The Museum of Modern Art, Extended Loan.*

104

Left: Les Réincarnations du Père Ubu. *1928. Etching, 12⅛ x 7¾". The Museum of Modern Art, Extended Loan.*

Right: *Pedagogue. 1931. Gouache, 14¼ x 10¾". Collection Dr. and Mrs. Harry Bakwin.*

Top: *Negro Porter. 1913–33. Gouache, 12¾ x 16⅞". Collection Dr. and Mrs. Harry Bakwin.*

Bottom: Les Réincarnations du Père Ubu. *1928. Etching, 8½ x 11⅞". The Museum of Modern Art, Extended Loan.*

106

Les Réincarnations du Père Ubu. *1928. Etching, 8½ x 11⅞". The Museum of Modern Art, Extended Loan.*

Left: Petite Banlieue: *Farniente. 1929. Lithograph, 13 x 8¾". The Museum of Modern Art, given anonymously.*

Right: Petite Banlieue: *Burial of Hope. 1929. Lithograph, 13 x 8¾". The Museum of Modern Art, given anonymously.*

108

Paysages Légendaires. 1929. Lithograph, 9⅛ x 6⅝". Collection Jean Goriany.

Left: Le Cirque. *1930. Color etching, 11¾ x 8⅞". The Museum of Modern Art, Extended Loan.*

Right: Le Cirque de L'Etoile Filante: *Master Arthur. 1934. Color etching, 12 x 8⅛". The Museum of Modern Art, Extended Loan.*

110

Left: Le Cirque de L'Etoile Filante: *Juggler. 1934. Color etching, 12⅛ x 8⅛″. The Museum of Modern Art, Extended Loan.*

Right: Le Cirque de L'Etoile Filante: *Weary Bones. 1934. Color etching, 12⅜ x 8⅛″. The Museum of Modern Art, Extended Loan.*

Left: Passion: *Plate V. 1935. Color etching, 11⅞ x 8⅜". The Museum of Modern Art, Extended Loan.*

Right: Passion: *Plate XVI. 1938. Color etching, 12¼ x 8½". The Museum of Modern Art, Extended Loan.*

Wood-engraving (1934) from the book, Passion *(1939). Executed by G. Aubert.*

CATALOG OF THE EXHIBITION

Paintings (Oil, Pastel, Gouache, Watercolor)

An asterisk (*) preceding the catalog number indicates that the work is illustrated.

* 1. THE ORDEAL OF SAMSON. 1893.
Oil on canvas, 57¾ x 44⅞".
Collection Mr. and Mrs. Maurice Sterne, Mount Kisco, N. Y. Ill. p. 33.

* 2. THE QUARRY. 1897.
Gouache and pastel, 32½ x 41".
Collection Mme. Henry Simon, Paris. Ill. p. 34.

* 3. HEAD OF YOUNG GIRL. 1904.
Oil and gouache, 9⅞ x 7⅝".
Collection Mr. and Mrs. Carl O. Schniewind, Chicago. Ill. p. 35.

* 4. BABEL. 1905–06 (?).
Oil, 23 x 31½".
Collection Miss Mary Rumsey, New York. Ill. p. 36.

* 5. WOMAN WITH RED STOCKINGS. 1905(?).
Gouache, 11⅞ x 7½".
Collection Albert Sarraut, Paris. Ill. p. 38.

* 6. WOMAN WITH A MIRROR. 1905.
Gouache, 9⅞ x 8¼".
Collection Dr. Girardin, Paris. Ill. p. 38.

* 7. NUDE. 1905.
Watercolor, 18 x 14½".
Private collection. Ill. p. 45.

* 8. COSTUMED MEN. 1906 (?).
Watercolor, 6⅞ x 4½".
Collection Leonard C. Hanna, Jr., Cleveland. Ill. p. 35.

* 9. NUDE TORSO. c. 1906.
Gouache, 15⅜ x 12¾".
The Art Institute of Chicago. Ill. p. 39.

* 10. THE SIRENS. 1906.
Gouache, 28 x 22¼".
Collection R. Sturgis Ingersoll, Philadelphia. Ill. p. 41.

* 11. CLOWN WITH THEATRE BOX. 1906.
Gouache and watercolor, 37¾ x 25¾".
Collection Mme. Henry Simon, Paris. Ill. p. 42.

* 12. CIRCUS WOMAN. 1906.
Pastel and gouache, 27 x 20".
Private collection. Ill. p. 43.

* 13. TWO PROSTITUTES. 1906.
Watercolor, 26½ x 24¼".
Collection Dr. and Mrs. Harry Bakwin, New York. Ill. p. 44.

* 14. WOMAN AT A TABLE. 1906.
Watercolor, 12½ x 9¼".
The Museum of Modern Art, acquired through the Lillie P. Bliss Bequest. Ill. p. 45.

15. CIRCUS. 1906.
Gouache, 14 x 17½".
Collection Mrs. Dudley Thayer, Weisel, Pa.

* 16. HEAD OF A CLOWN. c. 1907.
Oil on paper, 15½ x 12¼".
Private collection. Ill. p. 46.

* 17. CLOWN. c. 1907–08.
Oil on paper, 23⅝ x 18½".
The Dumbarton Oaks Research Library and Collection, Harvard University (Robert Woods Bliss Collection). Ill. p. 47.

* 18. THE JUDGES. c. 1907.
Oil on paper, 24¾ x 22¼".
The Portland Art Museum, Ore. Ill. p. 52.

* 19. THREE JUDGES. c. 1907.
Oil on paper, 14 x 22".
Collection Mr. and Mrs. Samuel A. Marx, Chicago. Ill. p. 52.

* 20. BATHERS. 1908.
Watercolor, 18 x 23½".
Collection Dr. and Mrs. MacKinley Helm, Brookline, Mass. Ill. p. 48.

* 21. BATHERS. 1908–10.
   Oil on composition board, 19 x 22″.
   Collection Mme. Carlos Martins, Washington,
   D. C. Ill. p. 49.

* 22. RED-HAIRED WOMAN. 1908.
   Gouache and watercolor, 27 x 19¼″.
   Collection Lt. and Mrs. Lee A. Ault, New Canaan,
   Conn. Ill. p. 50.

* 23. NUDE. 1909.
   Gouache and oil, 37⅞ x 25½″.
   Private collection. Ill. p. 51.

* 24. THE COURT. c. 1909.
   Oil on panel, 30¼ x 42⅛″.
   Collection Max Bangerter, Paris. Ill. p. 53.

* 25. PIERROT. 1910.
   Oil and pastel on paper, 33¼ x 19¼″.
   Collection Lt. and Mrs. Joseph Pulitzer, Jr.,
   St. Louis. Ill. p. 54.

* 26. HEAD OF A CLOWN. c. 1910.
   Gouache, 20 x 20″.
   Collection Dr. F. H. Hirschland, Harrison, N. Y.
   Ill. p. 55.

* 27. HEAD OF A WORKER. 1911.
   Oil on paper, 15½ x 11¼″.
   Collection Mr. and Mrs. Ralph F. Colin, New York.
   Ill. p. 56.

* 28. MAKE-UP, CIRQUE FORAIN. 1911.
   Oil and gouache, 14 x 11″.
   Collection Mme. Carlos Martins, Washington,
   D. C. Ill. p. 56.

* 29. MR. X. 1911.
   Oil on paper, 29½ x 21½″.
   Albright Art Gallery, Buffalo. Ill. p. 57.

* 30. HEAD OF A CLOWN. 1911.
   Ceramic, diameter 17⅝″.
   Collection Marcel Fleischmann, Zurich. Ill. p. 58.

* 31. HEAD OF CHRIST. c. 1911.
   Ceramic, diameter c. 15½″.
   Collection Walter Pach, New York. Ill. p. 58.

* 32. GROUP OF RUSTICS. 1911.
   Gouache and pastel, 28 x 25″.
   Pierre Matisse Gallery, New York. Ill. p. 61.

* 33. WOMAN AND CHILDREN. 1912.
   Gouache on cardboard, 12½ x 8⅝″.
   Collection Marcel Fleischmann, Zurich. Ill. p. 60.

* 34. WRESTLER. c. 1913.
   Gouache, 12 x 8″.
   Pierre Matisse Galley, New York. Ill. p. 60.

* 35. HEAD OF CHRIST. 1913.
   Oil on porcelain, 18¼ x 14¼″.
   Collection Miss Helen L. Resor, Greenwich, Conn.
   Ill. p. 62.

* 36. THREE JUDGES. 1913.
   Oil on canvas, 28⅜ x 40¼″.
   Collection Mr. and Mrs. Sam A. Lewisohn, New
   York. Color plate, opp p. 62.

  37. THE SHRIVELED BUCCANEER. 1913.
   Gouache, 10 x 5″.
   Collection Miss Marion G. Hendrie, Cincinnati.

* 38. THE COOK. 1914.
   Gouache on paper, 14 x 9¾″.
   Collection Mr. and Mrs. Sam A. Lewisohn, New
   York. Ill. p. 63.

* 39. THE LOVELY MADAM X. 1915.
   Gouache on paper, 13¾ x 9⅜″.
   Collection Mr. and Mrs. Sam A. Lewisohn, New
   York. Ill. p. 63.

* 40. THE CIRCUS TRAINER. 1915.
   Gouache, watercolor and crayon, 15½ x 10⅜″.
   Perls Galleries, New York. Ill. p. 64.

  41. PORTRAIT OF ANDRÉ SUARÈS. c. 1915(?).
   Watercolor and crayon, 11⅞ x 7½″.
   The Weyhe Gallery, New York.

  42. PORTRAIT OF A MAN. 1916.
   Crayon and watercolor, 12½ x 7¾″.
   Perls Galleries, New York.

* 43. HEAD. 1916.
   Gouache, 29½ x 22½″.
   Collection Walter Pach, New York.
   (On reverse of no. 44.) Ill. p. 66.

* 44. THE PALACE OF UBU ROI. 1916.
   Gouache, 29½ x 22½″.
   Collection Walter Pach, New York.
   (On reverse of no. 43.) Ill. p. 66.

* 45. THE PALACE OF UBU ROI. 1916.
   Gouache, 29 x 41½″.
   Collection Mr. and Mrs. Ralph M. Coe, Cleveland.
   Ill. p. 67.

* 46. Man with Spectacles. 1917.
Watercolor, 11¾ x 6½".
The Museum of Modern Art, gift of Mrs. John D.
Rockefeller, Jr. Ill. p. 64.

* 47. Portrait of Henri Lebasque. 1917.
Oil on canvas, 36¼ x 28⅞".
The Museum of Modern Art, Purchase Fund.
Ill. p. 65.

* 48. Three Clowns. 1917.
Oil on canvas, 41½ x 29½".
Collection Lt. and Mrs. Joseph Pulitzer, Jr.,
St. Louis. Ill. p. 69.

* 49. Clownerie. c. 1917.
Oil on canvas, 40½ x 28½".
Collection Lt. Wright Ludington, Santa Barbara,
Calif. Ill. p. 70.

* 50. Crucifixion. c. 1918.
Oil on canvas, 41¼ x 29⅝".
Collection Lt. Henry P. McIlhenny, U.S.N.R.,
Philadelphia. Ill. p. 71.

51. Dancers. c. 1918(?).
Gouache, 16 x 11½".
The Museum of Modern Art, given anonymously
(by exchange).

* 52. Circus Trio. c. 1924.
Oil on paper, 30 x 42".
The Phillips Memorial Gallery, Washington, D. C.
Ill. p. 72.

* 53. Grotesque. 1927.
Pastel, 12½ x 9".
Collection Werner Feuz, Clarens, Switzerland
(courtesy Lionello Venturi). Ill. p. 73.

* 54. Head of a Woman. 1927.
Pastel, 11 x 9".
Collection Werner Feuz, Clarens, Switzerland
(courtesy Lionello Venturi). Ill. p. 73.

55. Three Judges. 1928.
Oil, 29⅛ x 19⅛".
Collection Mr. and Mrs. Samuel A. Marx, Chicago.

* 56. Self Portrait. 1929.
Gouache, 20¼ x 14¼".
Collection Lt. and Mrs. Lee A. Ault, New Canaan,
Conn. Ill. p. 74.

* 57. Figure. 1929.
Oil, gouache and pastel on cardboard, 22 x 16¼".
Collection Bernard J. Reis, New York. Ill. p. 76.

* 58. At Gentilly. 1929.
Gouache and watercolor, 14 x 20".
Collection Elmer Rice, Stamford, Conn. Ill. p. 78.

* 59. Clown. 1930.
Oil, 11 x 8½".
Collection Miss Helen L. Resor, Greenwich, Conn.
Ill. p. 77.

* 60. Tragic Face. 1930.
Oil, 22 x 19¾".
Collection Mr. and Mrs. Sam A. Lewisohn, New
York. Ill. p. 79.

* 61. The Funeral. 1930.
Gouache and pastel, 11 x 19⅜".
The Museum of Modern Art, given anonymously.
Ill. p. 80.

* 62. Face to Face. c. 1930.
Oil and gouache on paper, 13¼ x 12¾".
Collection Mr. and Mrs. R. Kirk Askew, Jr., New
York. Ill. p. 80.

63. Man with Derby. 1930.
Gouache and pastel on paper, 18 x 11½".
Pierre Matisse Gallery, New York.

* 64. Afterglow, Galilee. c. 1930.
Oil on canvas, 19⅝ x 25½".
The Phillips Memorial Gallery, Washington, D. C.
Ill. p. 81.

* 65. Christ in Profile. 1930(?).
Oil on canvas, 28¾ x 23¾".
Collection Miss Mary E. Johnston, Glendale, Ohio.
Ill. p. 82.

* 66. Polichinelle. c. 1930.
Oil on paper, 28½ x 20".
Collection Mr. and Mrs. Walter C. Arensberg.
Hollywood. Ill. p. 83.

* 67. Pedagogue. 1931.
Gouache, 14¼ x 10¾".
Collection Dr. and Mrs. Harry Bakwin, New York.
Ill. p. 105.

* 68. Christ Mocked by Soldiers. 1932.
Oil on canvas, 36¼ x 28½".
The Museum of Modern Art, given anonymously.
Color plate, opp. p. 82.

* 69. Negro Porter. 1913–33.
Gouache, 12¾ x 16⅞".
Collection Dr. and Mrs. Harry Bakwin, New York.
Ill. p. 106.

* 70. WOMAN'S HEAD. c. 1936.
Oil on composition board, 31⅛ x 25¼".
Collection Marcel Fleischmann, Zurich. Ill. p. 84.

* 71. HEAD OF A CLOWN. c. 1936.
Oil on canvas, 9¾ x 7½".
Collection Mr. and Mrs. Vladimir Golschmann,
New York. Ill. p. 85.

72. HEAD OF PIERROT. 1936.
Oil on paper, 12¾ x 8½".
Collection Miss Agnes Rindge, Poughkeepsie.

* 73. DWARF. c. 1936.
Oil on canvas, 27⅛ x 19¾".
Bignou Gallery, New York. Ill. p. 86.

* 74. THE OLD KING. 1916–36.
Oil on canvas, 30¼ x 21¼".
Carnegie Institute, Pittsburgh. Color frontispiece.

* 75. PIERROT WITH A ROSE. c. 1936.
Oil on canvas, 36¾ x 24½".
Collection Mr. and Mrs. Samuel S. White, III,
Ardmore, Pa. Ill. p. 88.

* 76. THE LAST ROMANTIC. c. 1937.
Oil on wood, 26⅞ x 19¾".
Collection Dr. and Mrs. Harry Bakwin, New York.
Ill. p. 87.

* 77. BOUQUET. c. 1938.
Oil, 35 x 23¾".
Collection Mr. and Mrs. Ralph F. Colin, New
York. Ill. p. 89.

* 78. TURBANED WOMAN. 1939.
Oil on paper, 21¼ x 16".
Collection Lionello Venturi, New York. Ill. p. 90.

* 79. LANDSCAPE. 1939.
Oil on canvas, 16¼ x 22".
Collection Lionello Venturi, New York. Ill. p. 91.

* 80. NOCTURNE. 1939.
Oil, 28 x 39".
Collection Miss Mary E. Johnston, Glendale, Ohio.
Ill. p. 91.

* 81. THE WOUNDED CLOWN. 1939.
Oil, 71 x 46".
Private collection. Ill. p. 92.

Prints

Dimensions given are for the image in the case of lithographs, for the plate in the case of etchings.

Titles given in capitals are actual; if in quotation marks, merely descriptive.

Unless otherwise noted, prints listed are on Extended Loan to the Museum.

* 82. THE MONK. 1910(?).
Lithograph, 11⅞ x 8½".
Buchholz Gallery, New York. Ill. p. 94.

* 83. CLOWN WITH MONKEY. 1910.
Monotype, 22¼ x 15".
Collection Mr. and Mrs. Sam A. Lewisohn, New
York. Ill. p. 94.

* 84. THE HORSEMAN (*Le Conducteur de Chevaux*). 1910.
Color lithograph, 13⅛ x 17½".
The Brooklyn Museum, New York. Ill. p. 93.

* 85. THE HIDEOUS WOMAN. 1918.
Etching, 10¼ x 6⅝".
Collection Jean Goriany (courtesy The Art Institute of Chicago). Ill. p. 95.

* 86 THE HIDEOUS WOMAN. 1919.
Etching with aquatint, 12⅛ x 7¾".
Collection Jean Goriany (courtesy The Art Institute of Chicago). Ill. p. 95.

Miserere et Guerre. 1916-1927

Unpublished portfolio of prints, issued separately by Ambroise Vollard. The prints for Miserere et Guerre shown from the Museum Collection, Extended Loan, are all first trial proofs. Many of them have been retouched by the artist.

87. FACE TO FACE. 1920.
Etching, 22⅝ x 17⅛".

* 88. THE BLIND WILL LONG BE LED BY THE HALT. 1920.
Etching, 23⅛ x 17⅛".
Ill. p. 99.

89. ST. VERONICA'S VEIL. 1921 (?).
Etching, 17⅛ x 16⅞".

* 90. IN THE PRESS, THE GRAPE WAS TRAMPLED. 1922.
Etching, 15½ x 19".
Ill. p. 97.

91. SING MORNING PRAYERS—THE DAY IS REBORN.
1922.
Etching, 20⅛ x 14⅜".

92. THE CONDEMNED MAN HAS DEPARTED, INDIFFERENT AND WEARY. 1922.
Etching, 18⅞ x 14¼".

* 93. SOCIETY WOMAN. 1922.
Etching, 22½ x 16¼″.
Ill. p. 96.

* 94. TWO GROTESQUES. 1922.
Etching, 22⅜ x 16¼″.
Collection Jean Goriany (courtesy The Art Institute of Chicago). Ill. p. 96.

95. THE FAUBOURG OF LONG SUFFERING. 1922.
Etching, 14¼ x 20″.

96. JESUS, FOREVER FLAGELLATED. 1922.
Etching, 19 x 14⅜″.

97. HEAD OF CHRIST, BOWED TO RIGHT. 1922.
Etching, 22½ x 15¾″.

98. SORROWFUL WOMAN. 1922.
Etching, 20 x 16″.
The Art Institute of Chicago, gift of Chauncey McCormick.

* 99. WHO DOES NOT FROWN? 1923.
Etching, 22¼ x 16⅞″.
Ill. p. 102.

100. JEAN MARIE TERRENEUVUS, JEAN MARIE DOES NOT BELONG TO THE ACADEMY. 1923.
Etching, 23⅛ x 16⅝″.

101. LOVE YE ONE ANOTHER. 1926.
Etching, 22⅞ x 16⅜″.

102. DIG YOUR GRAVE, MY BOY—AND REST. 1926.
Etching, 23 x 16½″.

* 103. THE DEPOSITION. 1926.
Etching, 23 x 16½″.
Collection Miss Ann C. Resor, Greenwich, Con.
Ill. p. 98.

104. DURA LEX SED LEX. 1926.
Etching, 22½ x 17⅛″.

105. EURYDICE! EURYDICE! 1926.
Etching, 22¾ x 16⅜″.

* 106. LOUIS XI (Ambroise Vollard?). 1926 (?).
Etching, 22¾ x 16⅜″.
Collection Jean Goriany (courtesy The Art Institute of Chicago). Ill. p. 101.

107. THE BEGGAR. 1926 (?).
Etching and aquatint, retouched by the artist with color crayon and pastel, 24 x 18¼″.
Collection Frank B. Hubachek, Chicago.

* 108. WITH NEITHER LIFE NOR JOY. 1926.
Etching, 23 x 16⅝″.
Ill. p. 99.

* 109. THIS WILL BE THE LAST, LITTLE FATHER. 1927.
Etching, 23⅛ x 16⅞″.
Ill. p. 100.

110. IT IS YOU, MY LORD, I RECOGNIZE YOU. 1927.
Etching, 22⅜ x 17¾″.

111. FROM THE DEPTHS WE CRY TO THEE, O LORD. 1927.
Etching, 17 x 23⅝″.

112. WAR IS HORRIBLE FOR MOTHERS. 1927.
Etching, 23 x 17⅜″.

113. THE VERY DEAD ARE RISEN. 1927.
Etching, 23 x 17⅜″.

* 114. MAN IS A WOLF TO MAN. 1927.
Etching, 16⅝ x 23½″.
Ill. p. 97.

115. WOMAN WITH HAT. Not dated.
Etching, 24 x 18″.
Collection Mr. and Mrs. Ralph F. Colin, New York.

* 116. TENDERNESS.
Impression from photogravure plate before handwork was applied, 24⅛ x 16¼″.
The Art Institute of Chicago, Joseph Brooks Fair Collection. Ill. p. 30.

* 117. TENDERNESS. 1922.
Impression from plate after etching and aquatint were applied, 24⅛ x 16¼″.
The Art Institute of Chicago, Joseph Brooks Fair Collection. Ill. p. 30.

The Frapier Prints (c. 1924-1927)

Note from E. Frapier's catalog of 1926: "All our prints (52 x 37) are signed by the artist, numbered and stamped; since 1925 they have been marked with a symbol indicating their state."

ℰ Trial proof   ⚑ 1st state   ⚐ 2nd state

ℰ 3rd state   ⚑ 4th state

* 118. ACROBAT. c. 1925.
Lithograph, trial proof, 1st state, 12½ x 9″.
The Museum of Modern Art, given anonymously.

119. Carmencita.
Lithograph, trial proof, 2nd stone, 1st state,
13⅝ x 9".
The Brooklyn Museum, New York.

120. The Boxers, Cirque Forain.
Lithograph, trial proof, 1st stone, 2nd state,
13 x 8¼".
The Brooklyn Museum, New York.

121. Circus Rider.
Lithograph, trial proof, 4th state, 13⅜ x 8¾"
(remarque 2 x 1½").
The Museum of Modern Art, given anonymously.

122. The Juggler.
Lithograph, 3rd state, 12½ x 8¼".
Collection Jean Goriany (courtesy The Art Insti-
tute of Chicago).

123. Prostitute.
Lithograph, 2nd state, 12⅞ x 9".
The Museum of Modern Art, given anonymously.

* 124. The Strong Man.
Lithograph, trial proof, 2nd state, 13⅛ x 8⅞".
The Brooklyn Museum, New York. Ill. p. 103.

125. The Human Wreck (Le Pitre).
Lithograph, 13⅝ x 8⅞".
Collection Jean Goriany (courtesy The Art Insti-
tute of Chicago).

126. Flotsam.
Lithograph, trial proof, 1st state, 11⅞ x 8⅜".
The Museum of Modern Art, given anonymously.

* 127. Self Portrait with Cap.
Lithograph, 9⅛ x 6¾".
Buchholz Gallery, New York. Ill. p. 20.

* 128. André Suarès. 1926.
Lithograph, 9½ x 7".
Collection Jean Goriany (courtesy The Art Insti-
tute of Chicago). Ill. p. 20.

* 129. Léon Bloy.
Lithograph, 9¼ x 6½".
Collection Jean Goriany (courtesy The Art Insti-
tute of Chicago. Ill. p. 13.

130. Baudelaire. 1927.
Lithograph, 8⅜ x 6⅜" (remarque 1¾ x 1⅜").
The Museum of Modern Art, given anonymously.

* 131. Gustave Moreau (Moreau au Petit Chapeau).
Lithograph, 9 x 6¾".
The Museum of Modern Art, given anonymously.
Ill. p. 13.

132. J. K. Huysmans.
Lithograph, 9⅛ x 6¾".
Collection Jean Goriany (courtesy The Art Insti-
tute of Chicago).

133. Self Portrait. (Frapier ?). 1929.
Color lithograph, 13⅝ x 9¾".
The Museum of Modern Art, given anonymously.

Petite Banlieue (The Little Suburb)

Series of 6 lithographs. 100 sets, of which 2 were hand
colored by the artist. Paris, Editions Quatre Chemins, 1929.

* 134. Farniente. 1929.
Lithograph, 13 x 8¾".
The Museum of Modern Art, given anonymously.
Ill. p. 108.

* 135. Burial of Hope. 1929.
Lithograph, 13 x 8¾".
The Museum of Modern Art, given anonymously.
Ill. p. 108.

Paysages Légendaires

Poems by Rouault, illustrated by 6 lithographs and 50
drawings. Paris, Porteret, 1929.

136. "Two figures in a landscape." 1929.
Lithograph, 9½ x 6¾".
Collection Jean Goriany (courtesy The Art Insti-
tute of Chicago).

* 137. "Watteau." 1929.
Lithograph, 9⅛ x 6⅝".
Collection Jean Goriany (courtesy The Art Insti-
tute of Chicago). Ill. p. 109.

Les Carnets de Gilbert

Text by Marcel Arland, illustrated by 1 lithograph and 8
facsimiles of gouaches (5 in color and 3 in sepia). Paris,
NRF, 1931.

138. Lithograph. 1930.
10⅜ x 7 1/16".
Collection Glenway Westcott, Hampton, N. J.

Les Réincarnations du Père Ubu

Text by Ambroise Vollard, illustrated with 22 etchings and
104 wood-engravings (engraved by Georges Aubert). Paris,
Vollard, 1932.

* 139. "Landscape with road." 1928.
Etching, 11⅝ x 7⅜".
Ill. p. 104.

140. "Man with hat and white shirt." 1928.
Etching, 11¾ x 7⅝".

* 141. "Two women in profile." 1928.
  Etching, 10⅝ x 7⅜".
  Ill. p. 104.

  142. "The lovers." 1928.
  Etching, 12⅛ x 8¾".

* 143. "Dragon." 1928.
  Etching, 8½ x 11⅞".
  Ill. p. 107.

* 144. "Negro porter." 1928.
  Etching, 8½ x 11⅞".
  Ill. p. 106.

* 145. "Pedagogue." 1928.
  Etching, 12⅛ x 7¾".
  Ill. p. 105.

* Also 2 gouache studies for nos. 144 and 145, as listed in painting section. Ill. pp. 105, 106.

Le Cirque

Text by André Suarès, illustrated with 7 color etchings and 82 wood-engravings. Unpublished, Paris, Vollard, 1938.

  146. "Seated clown, facing spectator." 1930.
  Color etching, 12⅞ x 9".

* 147. "Equestrienne." 1930.
  Color etching, 11¾ x 8⅞".
  Ill. p. 110.

Le Cirque de L'Etoile Filante

Text by Rouault, illustrated with 17 color etchings and 82 wood-engravings (engraved by Georges Aubert). Paris, Vollard, 1938.

  148. PARADE. 1934.
  Color etching, 12⅛ x 7¾".

* 149. JUGGLER. 1934.
  Color etching, 12⅛ x 8⅛".
  Ill. p. 111.

* 150. WEARY BONES. 1934.
  Color etching, 12⅜ x 8⅛".
  Ill. p. 111.

* 151. MASTER ARTHUR. 1934.
  Color etching, 12 x 8⅛".
  Ill. p. 110.

Passion

Text by André Suarès, illustrated with 17 color etchings and 82 wood-engravings (engraved by Georges Aubert). Paris, Vollard, 1939.

  152. Frontispiece. 1935.
  Color etching, 12¼ x 8¾".

* 153. Plate V. 1935.
  Color etching, 11⅞ x 8⅜".
  Ill. p. 113.

  154. Plate VI. 1936.
  Color etching, 12¾ x 8⅛".

* 155. Plate XVI. 1938.
  Color etching, 12¼ x 8½".
  Ill. p. 113.

Ballet

Le Fils Prodigue (The Prodigal Son). Ballet in one act of three scenes. Book: Boris Kochno. Music: Serge Prokofiev. Choreography: George Balanchine. Presented by Serge de Diaghilev at the Théâtre Sarah Bernhardt, Paris, May 21, 1929.

* 156. Décor. 1929.
  Watercolor, 20¼ x 28¾".
  Wadsworth Atheneum, Hartford. Ill. p. 75.

* 157. Décor. 1929.
  Watercolor, 20 x 28¼".
  Wadsworth Atheneum, Hartford. Ill. p. 75.

Tapestries

* 158. THE DANCER. 1931.
  Wool tapestry, 89¾ x 50½".
  Collection Mme. Marie Cuttoli, Paris (courtesy San Francisco Museum of Art). Ill. p. 27.

* 159. WOUNDED CLOWN. 1931.
  Wool tapestry, 76⅝ x 46⅛".
  Collection Mme. Marie Cuttoli, Paris (courtesy San Francisco Museum of Art). Ill. p. 27.

* 160. ST. VERONICA'S VEIL. 1932.
  Wool tapestry, 32½ x 28½".
  Collection Mme. Marie Cuttoli, Paris (courtesy San Francisco Museum of Art). Ill. p. 28.

  161. LES FLEURS DU MAL. c. 1932.
  Wool tapestry, 43 x 29⅜".
  Collection Mme. Marie Cuttoli, Paris (courtesy San Francisco Museum of Art).

1. Jacques Maritain, "Léon Bloy." *The Colosseum*, vol. III, no. 9, London, Mar. 1936, p. 16.

2. Georges Rouault, *Souvenirs Intimes*. Paris, E. Frapier, 1926, p. 58.

3. Robert Speaight, "Homage to Rouault." *The Dublin Review*, vol. 209, July 1941, p. 60.

4. Jacques Maritain, *Art and Poetry*. New York, The Philosophical Library, 1943, p. 23.

5. Georges Rouault, *Souvenirs Intimes*. Paris, E. Frapier, 1926, p. 81.

6. Ambroise Vollard, *Recollections of a Picture Dealer*. Boston, Little, Brown & Co., 1936, pp. 213-214.

7. Robert Speaight, "Homage to Rouault." *The Dublin Review*, vol. 209, July 1941, p. 63.

8. Georges Rouault, *Souvenirs Intimes*. Paris, E. Frapier, 1926, p. 98.

9. *Ibid*, p. 82.

10. Jerome Mellquist, "Rouault, Prophet of Disaster." *The Commonweal*, vol. 36, New York, Aug. 14, 1942, p. 390.

11. James Johnson Sweeney, "The Period of Gustave Moreau and the New Century." (A lecture delivered at the Frick Collection, New York, 1940.)

12. André Suarès, "Gustave Moreau" ("Lettre d'André Suarès à Rouault"). *L'Art et les Artistes*, vol. 20, Paris, April 1926, p. 218.

13. Georges Rouault, *Souvenirs Intimes*. Paris, E. Frapier, 1926, p. 34.

14. Georges Rouault, "Gustave Moreau" (Lettres de Rouault à Suarès"). *L'Art et les Artistes*, vol. 20. Paris, April 1926, p. 246.

15. Michel Puy, *Georges Rouault*, ("Peintres français nouveaux"). Paris, Librairie Gallimard, 1920, p. 15.

16. Léon Bloy, *La Femme Pauvre*. Paris, Mercure de France, 1937 (32nd edition), p. 171.

17. *Ibid*, p. 299.

18. Georges Rouault, *Souvenirs Intimes*. Paris, E. Frapier, 1926, p. 58.

19. *Ibid*, p. 57.

20. André Suarès, "Gustave Moreau" ("Lettre d'André Suarès à Rouault"). *L'Art et les Artistes*, vol. 20, Paris, April 1926, p. 218.

21. *Ibid*, p. 218.

22. Ernest Hello, *L'Homme*. Paris, Librairie Académique Perrin, 1936 (36th edition), p. 19.

23. *Ibid.*, p. 328.

24. *Ibid.*, p. 356.

25. Stanislas Fumet, *Mission de Léon Bloy*. Paris, Desclée de Brouwer, 1935, p. 144.

26. Joseph Bollery, 'Le Désespéré' de Léon Bloy. Paris, Société Française d'Editions Littéraires et Techniques, 1937, p. 127.

27. Lionello Venturi, *Georges Rouault*. New York, E. Weyhe, 1940, p. 16.

28. *Ibid.*, p. 16.

29. Léon Bloy, *La Femme Pauvre*. Paris, Mercure de France, 1937 (32nd edition), p. 76.

30. *Ibid.*, p. 75.

31. Raïssa Maritain, *We Have Been Friends Together*. New York, Longmans, Green & Co., 1942, p. 158.

32. Georges Charensol, *Georges Rouault*. Paris, Editions des Quatres Chemins, 1926, p. 23.

33. Georges Rouault, "Gustave Moreau: A Propos de Son Centenaire." *Le Correspondant*, 303, Paris, April 10, 1926, p. 142.

34. Robert Speaight, "Homage to Rouault." *The Dublin Review*, vol. 209, July 1941, p. 66.

35. Georges Rouault, "Gustave Moreau" ("Lettres de Rouault à Suarès"). *L'Art et les Artistes*, vol. 20, Paris, April 1926, p. 222.

36. *Ibid.*, p. 242.

37. Robert Speaight, "Homage to Rouault." *The Dublin Review*, vol. 209, July 1941, p. 65.

38. *Gustave Moreau*. Paris, Librairie Centrale des Beaux-Arts, n.d., p. 5.

39. Jacques Maritain, *Art and Poetry*. New York, The Philosophical Library, 1943, p. 26.

40. Jacques Maritain, "Léon Bloy." *The Colosseum*, vol. III, no. 9, London, Mar. 1936, p. 14.

41. Georges Rouault, *Souvenirs Intimes*. Paris, E. Frapier, 1926, p. 83.

42. Claude Roulet, *Le Peintre Français: Georges Rouault*. Neuchâtel, Delachaux et Niestlé, 1937, p. 30.

43. Jerome Mellquist, "Georges Rouault: Christian Painter." *The Commonweal*, vol. 29, New York, Dec. 23, 1938, p. 233.

44. Letter from the artist to Pierre Matisse, New York.

45. Léon Bloy, *La Femme Pauvre*. Paris, Mercure de France, 1937 (32nd edition), p. 147.

46. Stanislas Fumet, *Mission de Léon Bloy*. Paris, Desclée de Brouwer, 1935, p. 143.

47. Georges Rouault, "Gustave Moreau" ("Lettres de Rouault à Suarès"). *L'Art et les Artistes*, vol. 20, Paris, April 1926, p. 242.

48. James Johnson Sweeney, "Carnegie International 1938." *Parnassus*, Nov. 1938, p. 15.

49. Robert Speaight, "Homage to Rouault." *The Dublin Review*, vol. 209, July 1941, p. 60.

50. Ernest Hello, *L'Homme*. Paris, Librairie Académique Perrin, 1936 (36th edition), p. 36.

51. Monroe Wheeler, *The Prints of Georges Rouault*. The Museum of Modern Art, 1938, p. 7.

52. Georges Rouault, *Souvenirs Intimes*. Paris, E. Frapier, 1926, p. 84.

53. Daniel Théote, "Intimate Moments with Rouault: Three Wars." *Tricolor*, vol. I, no. 2, New York, May 1944, p. 83.

54. Jacques Maritain, "Léon Bloy." *The Colosseum*, vol. III, no. 9, London, Mar. 1936, p. 12.

55. Alfred Jarry, letter to Lugné-Poé (quoted from *Ubu Roi*, Paris, Fasquelle, n.d., p. 16).

56. Georges Rouault, *Souvenirs Intimes*. Paris, E. Frapier, 1926, p. 82.

57. Monroe Wheeler, *The Prints of Georges Rouault*. The Museum of Modern Art, 1938, p. 7.

58. Léon Deshairs, preface to *Gustave Moreau*. Paris, Librairie Centrale des Beaux-Arts, n.d., p. 14.

59. Marcel Arland, "About Georges Rouault." *Formes*, no. 16, Paris, June 1931, p. 96.

60. *Art in Australia*, series IV, no. 2, June-Aug., 1941, p. 28.

61. Georges Rouault, *Souvenirs Intimes*. Paris, E. Frapier, 1926, pp. 75-76.

62. *Ibid.*, p. 76.

63. Gladys Delmas, "French Art During the Occupation,"*Magazine of Art*,Washington, D. C., Mar. 1945.

BIBLIOGRAPHY

In the preparation of the following, all known published lists of works on Rouault have been consulted (see bibl. 40,54,83,102,170,189), the most extensive being the compilations contained in Venturi's book (189) and in the catalog of the Boston Institute of Modern Art (40). Omitted here are some references to articles in French journals mentioned by Venturi and to some exhibition notices listed in Art Index. All material, except items marked with †, has been examined by the compiler. References preceded by * are in the Museum Library.

ABBREVIATIONS. Ag August, Ap April, D December, ed editor, F February, il illustration(s), Ja January, Je June, Jy July, Mr March, My May, N November, ns new series, no number(s), O October, p page(s), por portrait(s), S September, sup supplement(ary).

SAMPLE ENTRY for magazine article. ARLAND, MARCEL. About Georges Rouault. 6il Formes no16:96-7 Je 1931.

EXPLANATION. An article by Marcel Arland, entitled "About Georges Rouault", containing 6 illustrations, will be found in Formes, number 16, pages 96 to 97 inclusive, the June 1931 issue.

HANNAH B. MULLER

Writings by Rouault

1 À LA MÉMOIRE DE CLAUDE MONET [poem] Amour de l'Art 8:201 1927.

2 ANDRÉ DERAIN. Chroniques du Jour 8:3 Ja 1931. Rouault's comments on being asked to criticize the work of Derain. His reply is not critical, but a protest against the nature of the question.

* 3 L'ARTISTE. MISERERE. MÈRE [poems] Soirées de Paris 3no26-7:432-4 Jy-Ag 1914.

* 4 LE CIRQUE DE L'ÉTOILE FILANTE. 168p 99il Paris, Vollard, 1938.

5 CLAUDE MONET. Amour de l'Art 8:200 1927.

6 CLIMAT PICTURAL. 1il Renaissance 20:3-4 O-D 1937.

7 GEORGES ROUAULT RÉPOND À NOTRE ENQUÊTE SUR LE MÉTIER. 2il Beaux Arts 74no198:5 O 1936.

8 DEUX POÈMES DE GEORGES ROUAULT: LE CHRIST DE L'YSER. HOMMAGE AU SOLITAIRE. 2il Amour de l'Art 6:445-6 N 1925.

9 ÉVOCATIONS [SUR MATISSE] Chroniques du Jour 9:8-9 Ap 1931.

* 10 LES FRONTIÈRES ARTISTIQUES. *In* Les appels de l'Orient. p177-82 Paris, Émile-Paul frères, 1925. (Les cahiers du mois 9/10)

11 GEORGES ROUAULT POÈTE. 2il Bulletin de la Vie Artistique 5no17:380-4 S 1 1924.

12 GUSTAVE MOREAU. Correspondant (Paris) 303 (ns267):141-3 Ap 10 1926.

* 13 UNE LETTRE DE GEORGES ROUAULT [À CHRISTIAN ZERVOS] Cahiers d'Art 3no3:102 1928.

14 LETTRES DE GEORGES ROUAULT À ANDRÉ SUARÈS. Art et les Artistes 20(ns13):219-48 Ap 1926. Letters written in memory of Gustave Moreau.

† 15 PAYSAGES LÉGENDAIRES. Paris, Porteret, 1929.

* 16 PICTORIAL CONCEITS. 2il Verve 2no4:104-6 Ja-Mr 1939.

17 [POÈMES] 1il Bulletin de la Vie Artistique 6no6:127-30 Mr 15 1925.

18 PRÉFACE. *In* Sullivan, Mrs. Cornelius J., Galleries, New York. An. Girard—exhibition of paintings. p3-5 1938.

* 19 [RÉPONSE À L'ENQUÊTE SUR L'ART D'AUJOURD' HUI] Cahiers d'Art 10:11-18 1935.

20 RÉPONSE À L'ENQUÊTE: L'ART, PEUT-IL UTILISER LA PHOTOGRAPHIE? Revue de l'Art Ancien et Moderne 69:88 Mr 19 1936.

† 21 SOLILOQUES. Avant propos de Claude Roulet.196p 8il Neuchâtel, Aux Ides et Calendes, 1944.

† 21a SOUVENIRS DU JEUNE AGE SONT GRAVÉS DANS MON COEUR. Le Point 5no26-7 Ag-O 1943.

22 SOUVENIRS INTIMES. 99p 6il Paris, E. Frapier, 1926.

23 TROIS ARTISTES: *"Noli Me Tangere"* (CÉZANNE); *La Toison D'Or* (CARRIÈRE); *Le Grand Pan* (RODIN) Mercure de France 83:654-9 F 16 1910.

* 24 VISAGE DE LA FRANCE. 5col il Verve 2no8:12-21 S-N 1940.

* 25 VISAGES RÉELS OU IMAGINAIRES. Verve 2no5-6 Jy-O 1939.

See Also bibl. 40, 47, 48, 82, 97, 104, 105, 107, 155, 158, 170, 182, 183.

Literature on Rouault

* 26 ARLAND, MARCEL. About Georges Rouault. 6il Formes no16:96-7 Je 1931.

27 —— Premier regard sur l'exposition des Maîtres de l'Art Indépendant. Nouvelle Revue Française 49:350-2 Ag 1937.
"Rouault" p352.

* 28 ARTS CLUB OF CHICAGO. Catalog of an exhibition of paintings by Georges Rouault. 3p lil 1930.
—— See also 67.

BARR, ALFRED H., JR. See 144.

29 BASEL. KUNSTHALLE. Vlaminck, R. Dufy, Rouault. 30p 1938.
"Georges Rouault" p17-22, with introduction reprinted from Vlaminck's Désobéir.

† 29a BASLER, ADOLPHE. Rue de Seine. 4il Kunstblatt 14:310-11 O 1930.

* 30 —— & KUNSTLER, CHARLES. Modern French painting: the modernists from Matisse to De Segonzac. p30-1 2il New York, W. F. Payson, 1931.
Translation of La peinture indépendante en France. Paris, Crès, 1929.

31 BELL, CLIVE. [Rouault exhibition at Mayor Gallery] New Statesman and Nation ns10:558 O 19 1935.

* 32 BENSON, EMANUEL MERVIN. Of many things. 2il Magazine of Art 27:20-2 Ja 1934.
Exhibition, Pierre Matisse Gallery.

33 BERTHELOT, PIERRE. Rouault. Beaux Arts 8:24 Ag 25 1931.
Exhibition, Galerie des Quatre Chemins.

BESSON, GEORGE. See 158a.

34 BIGNOU GALLERY, NEW YORK. Modern French tapestries . . . from the collection of Madame Paul Cuttoli. p18-20 1il 1936.
Exhibition catalog.

35 —— Paintings and gouaches by Georges Rouault. 11p 5il 1940.
Exhibition catalog.

36 BINSSE, HARRY LORIN. [Painter of religious subjects] America 63:165 My 18 1940.

* 37 BLOY, LÉON. Notes de Léon Bloy sur Rouault. Cahiers d'Art 3no3:102,104 1928.
Reprinted from the author's L'Invendable.
—— See also other writings of Bloy for references to Georges Rouault.

38 BLUNT, ANTHONY. Matisse and Rouault. Spectator 159:144 Jy 23 1937.
Exhibition, Mayor Gallery.

39 —— Rouault. Spectator 155:607 O 18 1935.

* 40 BOSTON. INSTITUTE OF MODERN ART. Georges Rouault: retrospective loan exhibition. 96p 58il 1940.
Exhibition catalog with introduction by Lionello Venturi, facsimile of letter by Rouault, 1939, bibliography and list of exhibitions. Reprinted in part in catalog issued by Marie Harriman Gallery. 66p 28il 1941.

* 41 BREUNING, MARGARET. [Georges Rouault exhibition] Parnassus 9:22-4 D 1937.
Exhibition, Pierre Matisse Gallery.

* 42 BRUMMER GALLERY, NEW YORK. Rouault: exhibition. 3p 1930.
Exhibition catalog.

* 43 BUCHHOLZ GALLERY, NEW YORK. Lithographs & etchings, Georges Rouault. folded sheet 8il 1940.
Exhibition announcement with reproductions from Rouault's Le cirque de l'étoile filante, and text by Monroe Wheeler reprinted from Museum of Modern Art catalog: The prints of Georges Rouault.

* 44 BULLIET, CLARENCE JOSEPH. Apples & madonnas. p152-3 Chicago, Covici-Friede, 1927.

* 45 CARCO, FRANCIS. Le nu dans la peinture moderne. p134-6 1il Paris, Crès, 1924.
Includes quotation of comment by Jean Pellerin on occasion of Rouault's exhibition at Galerie La Licorne, 1920.

* 46 CHABOT, GEORGES. Georges Rouault. 7il Cahiers d'Art 3no3:104-12 1928.

47 —— Georges Rouault. 10il Revue d'Art (Antwerp) 45:101-16 S 1928.
Includes quotations from Rouault's writings. Article also reprinted as separate and published

with two lithographs as part of series: Études d'art contemporain.

* 48 CHARENSOL, GEORGES. Georges Rouault, l'homme et l'oeuvre. 36p 40il Paris, Éditions des Quatre Chemins, 1926.

Includes "lettre-préface" and 2 poems by Rouault. An extract appears in Art Vivant 2:128-30 F 15 1926, and the letter is reprinted, accompanied by 2il, in Kunstblatt 11:303-6 Ag 1927. †

* 49 THE CHARTRES COLOR OF GEORGES ROUAULT. 1il Art Digest 13:20 F 15 1939.
Exhibition, Pierre Matisse Gallery.

* 50 CHENEY, SHELDON. Expressionism in art. passim 5il New York, Liveright, 1934.

*, 51 —— The story of modern art. p358-60,484-6 3il New York, Viking press, 1941.

* 52 CLOT, RENÉ-JEAN. Sur deux bouches: [Sainte Anne de Léonard de Vinci; Le Juge de Rouault] 2il Prométhée 20:65-6 Ap 1939.

* 53 COATES, ROBERT M. Rouault and some others. New Yorker 17:71 Ap 26 1941.
Exhibition, Marie Harriman Gallery.

* 54 COGNIAT, RAYMOND. Georges Rouault. 14p 32il Paris, Crès, 1930. (Collection "Les artistes nouveaux")
Includes bibliography.

55 —— Georges Rouault. 6il Chroniques du Jour 6:3-5 My 1930.

56 —— Georges Rouault. 2il Le Point 2no3:115-16 O 1937.

57 —— Georges Rouault et Ambroise Vollard. 1il Beaux Arts 72no23:6 Je 9 1933.

† 57a —— Theaterdekorationen der Avantgarde in Frankreich. 1il Kunstblatt 14:250,253 Ag 1930.

* 58 COQUIOT, GUSTAVE. Cubistes, futuristes, passéistes. p156-60 1il Paris, Ollendorff, 1914.

† 59 —— Des peintres maudits. Paris, Delpeuch, 1924.
Chapter on Rouault.

* 60 —— Les indépendants, 1884-1920. 4e éd. p72-3 1il Paris, Ollendorff [1920?]

* 61 COURTHION, PIERRE. Panorama de la peinture française contemporaine. 3e éd. p123-31 2il Paris, S. Kra, 1927.

62 COUTURIER, FRÈRE M. A. Rouault et le public ecclésiastique. 4il Art Sacré (Paris) 4no33:244-7 S 1938.

* 63 DALZELL HATFIELD GALLERIES, LOS ANGELES. Rouault. 3p 1il 1940.
Exhibition catalog.

* 64 DAVIDSON, MARTHA. Old and new paintings by Rouault, a twentieth century visionary. 1il Art News 37:11 F 11 1939.
Exhibition, Pierre Matisse Gallery.

* 65 —— Rouault as a master of graphic art. 2il Art News 37:10,20 O 8 1938.
Exhibition, Museum of Modern Art.

* 66 —— Rouault: stained glass in paint. 1il Art News 36:8,18 N 20 1937.
Exhibition, Pierre Matisse Gallery.

* 67 DEMOTTE, NEW YORK. Paintings by Georges Rouault. 4p 1il 1931.
Exhibition catalog. Same paintings and three others listed in catalog issued by Arts Club of Chicago. 3p 1il 1931.

* 68 DORMOY, MARIE. Cirque de l'étoile filante de Georges Rouault. 8il Arts et Métiers Graphiques no68:35-40 My 15 1939.

* 69 —— Georges Rouault. 8il Kunst und Künstler 29:280-6 Ap 1931.

* 70 —— Georges Rouault. 13il Arts et Métiers Graphiques no48:23-30 Ag 15 1935.

71 —— Georges Rouault tel que je l'ai vu. 5il Renaissance 20:30-2 O-D 1937.

72 DRUET, E., GALERIE, PARIS. Exposition de peintures et de céramiques de G. Rouault. 18p 1il 1910.
Exhibition catalog with introduction by Jacques Favelle.

73 —— Oeuvres de Georges Rouault de 1897 à 1919. 8p 1924.
Exhibition catalog.

* 74 DU COLOMBIER, PIERRE & MANUEL, ROLAND. Les arts. p51-2 Paris, Denoël et Steele, 1933. (Tableau du XXe siècle (1900-1933) I)
Includes statement by Rouault, 1905.

75 EARP, THOMAS WADE. Rouault. New Statesman 35:335 Je 21 1930.

* 76 EINSTEIN, CARL. Georges Rouault. 9il Querschnitt 5hft3:244-8 Mr 1925.

* 77 —— Die Kunst des 20. Jahrhunderts. 2. Auflage. p49-50, 249-55 7il Berlin, Propyläen Verlag, 1926. (Propyläen-Kunstgeschichte, XVI)

* 78 ESCHOLIER, RAYMOND. La peinture française XXe siècle. p31-5 7il(1 col) Paris, Floury, 1937.

* 79 EVALUATION OF ROUAULT. Art Digest 8-12 N 15 1933.
Digest of reviews of exhibition, Pierre Matisse Gallery.

80 EXHIBITION, BRUMMER GALLERY. Art Digest 4:16 Ap 15 1930.

* 81 EXHIBITION REVEALS ROUAULT'S PERSONALITY. 1il Art Digest 8:13 N 1 1933.
Exhibition, Pierre Matisse Gallery.

FAVELLE, JACQUES. See 72.

* 82 FELS, FLORENT. Propos d'artistes. p149-57 2il Paris, La Renaissance du Livre, 1925.
Prose and poetry by Rouault, p150-7. Reprinted with some revision and additional poems from Nouvelles Littéraires, Artistiques et Scientifiques p4 Mr 15 1924.

* 83 FIERENS, PAUL. Georges Rouault. *In* Huyghe, René, ed. Histoire de l'art contemporain; la peinture. p137-40 6il Paris, Alcan, 1935.
Includes bibliography. First published in Amour de l'Art 14:137-40 Je 1933.

* 84 FLINT, R. Georges Rouault. Art News 29:9 Ja 10 1931.
Exhibition, Demotte Galleries.

* 85 FRANKFURTER, ALFRED M. The full stature of Rouault. 9il Art News 39:1,6-9,16 N 9 1940.
Exhibition, Boston Institute of Modern Art.

* 86 —— Rouault: recent work. 2il Art News 38:12,16 My 11 1940.
Exhibition, Buchholz Gallery, Bignou Gallery.

* 87 FRY, ROGER. Transformations. p24-5,207-9 1il New York, Brentano's, 1926.

88 —— La peinture moderne en France. Amour de l'Art 5:141-60 1924.
"Rouault" p154,156-7, 1il.

89 GAUTHIER, MAXIMILIEN. Notices bio-bibliographiques des peintures figurant à l'exposition de l'Art Vivant. 3il Art Vivant 6:410,417,421 My 15 1930.

90 GEORGE, WALDEMAR. Georges Rouault. 1il Bulletin de la Vie Artistique 5no10:229-30 My 15 1924.
Reprinted from Paris-Journal.

* 91 —— Georges Rouault. 8il The Arts 9:317-24 Je 1926.

* 92 —— Georges Rouault and the birth of tragedy. 4il Formes no13:41 Mr 1931.

† 92a —— Georges Rouault: ein romantischer französischer Maler. 5il Kunstblatt 9:225-31 Ag 1925.

93 —— Georges Rouault, peintre sacré et maudit. 39il Renaissance 20:5-29 O-D 1937.
Excerpt reprinted in Beaux Arts 75no259:1,4 D 17 1937.
—— See also 142.

* 94 GEORGES-MICHEL, MICHEL. Peintres et sculpteurs que j'ai connus. p60-1 1il New York, Brentano's, 1942.

* 95 GEORGES ROUAULT. 1il Art News 28:10 Ap 5 1930.
Exhibition, Brummer Galleries.

* 96 GEORGES ROUAULT. 1il por Artlover, ed. by J. B. Neumann 3no2:17-19 [1930]

* 97 GEORGES ROUAULT. 4il(1 col) Art in Australia ser4no2:28-32 Je-Ag 1941.
Includes quotations from Rouault's writings.

98 GEORGES ROUAULT AT THE REDFERN GALLERY. New Statesman & Nation 20:136 Ag 10 1940.

99 GILLET, LOUIS. Trente ans de peinture au Petit Palais. Revue des Deux Mondes 107:319-39 Jy 15 1937.
"Deux artistes mystiques: Georges Desvallières et Georges Rouault" p336-8.

* 100 GOODRICH, LLOYD. Rouault. The Arts 17:120 N 1930.
Exhibition, Neumann Gallery.

* 101 GORDON, JAN. Modern French painters. p89-90 1il New York, Dodd, Mead, 1923.

102 GROHMANN, WILL. Rouault. *In* Thieme, Ulrich and Becker, Felix. Allgemeines Lexikon der bildenden Künstler, hrsg. von Hans Vollmer.29:106 Leipzig, E.A. Seemann, 1935.
—— See also 141.

HARRIMAN, MARIE, GALLERY, NEW YORK. See 40.

* 103 "HOMAGE TO ROUAULT." Carnegie Magazine 15:150 O 1941.
For the most part a reprint of a portion of Speaight's article in Dublin Review 209:59-68 Jy 1941 dealing with *The Old King* owned by Carnegie Institute.

104 HONE, EVIE. Georges Rouault. Liturgical Arts 11:87-8 Ag 1943.
Reprinted from Irish Ecclesiastical Record, F 1943. Includes quotation from writings of Rouault.

* 105 HUYGHE, RENÉ. La peinture française: les contemporains. p26-7 3il(1 col) Paris, Bibliothèque Française des Arts, 1939.
Includes quotations from writings of Rouault.

* 106 ITO, R. Rouault. 8p 37il(6 col) Tokio, Atelier-Sha, 1936.
Text in Japanese.

* 107 JOHNSON, UNA E. Ambroise Vollard editeur . . . an appreciation and catalogue. p27-31,37-8,137-50 8il New York, Wittenborn, 1944.
Includes facsimile of letter from Rouault to Vollard, Ja 1918.

108 KAHN, GUSTAVE. [Georges Rouault] Mercure de France 95:409 Ja 16 1912.
Exhibition, Galerie Druet.

† 108a KÁLLAI, ERNST. Dämonie der Satire. 1il Kunstblatt 11:102-3 Mr 1927.

* 109 KLEIN, JEROME. A mediaeval modern. New Freeman 1:255-7 My 24 1930.

KUNSTLER, ADOLPHE. See 30.

110 L., J. Rouault. 1il Beaux Arts 76no322:4 Mr 3 1939.
Exhibition, Galerie O. Pétridès.

* 111 LANE, JAMES W. Georges Rouault. 2il(1 col) Art News 40:27 Ap 15 1941.
Exhibition, Marie Harriman Gallery.

112 LAPRADE, JACQUES DE. Georges Rouault. Beaux Arts 74no163:8 F 14 1936.
Exhibition, Galerie Du Portique.
—— See also 158a.

113 LEHMANN, LÉON. Georges Rouault. por Beaux Arts 79no136:2 Ag 9 1935.
—— See also 158a.

114 LEICESTER GALLERIES, LONDON. Catalogue of an exhibition of paintings and gouaches by Rouault. 4p 1938.

* 115 LÉON-MARTIN, LOUIS. Georges Rouault. 9il Art et Décoration 57:111-18 Ap 1930.

* 116 LEWISOHN, SAM A. Rouault—master of dissonance. 10il Parnassus 5no6:1-7 N 1933.
Reprinted with editorial revision in the author's Painters and personality. p112-24 4il New York, Harper, 1937.

* 117 —— Drama in painting. Creative Art 9:185-98 S 1931.
"Rouault" p195-6; 2il p186.

* 118 LHOTE, ANDRÉ. Georges Rouault. 4il Cicerone 17hft3:132-6 F 1925.

* 119 —— La peinture: le coeur et l'esprit. p212-14 Paris, Denoël et Steele, 1933.

120 —— Rouault. 6il Amour de l'Art 4:779-82 D 1923.
Reprinted in the author's Parlons peinture. p257-62 Paris, Denoël et Steele, 1936.

121 LO DUCA, G. M. La pittura di G. Rouault. 1il Emporium 88:223 O 1938.
Exhibition, Galerie Zak.

* 122 McBRIDE, HENRY. The palette knife. Creative Art 6:sup111-12 My 1930.
Comment on the character of Rouault.

123 McCAUSLAND, ELIZABETH. [Rouault exhibition at Smith College] Springfield Sunday Union and Republican (Mass.) p6 N 17 1935.

124 —— [Rouault exhibition at Matisse Gallery] Springfield Sunday Union and Republican (Mass.) p6 N 21 1937.

125 —— [Rouault exhibition at Bignou Gallery] Springfield Sunday Union and Republican (Mass.) p6 F 2 1938.

126 —— [Rouault exhibition at Museum of Modern Art] Springfield Sunday Union and Republican (Mass.) p6 O 2 1938.

* 127 —— [Rouault exhibition at Bignou Gallery] Parnassus 12:40 My 1940.

* 128 —— Rouault exhibition at Marie Harriman's. Springfield Sunday Union and Republican (Mass.) p6 Ap 27 1941.

* 129 McGREEVY, THOMAS. Georges Rouault. London Studio 17(Studio 117):271 Je 1939.
Exhibition, Zwemmer Gallery.

* 130 MALREAUX, ANDRÉ. Notes on tragic expression in painting apropos of the recent work of Rouault. 17il(1 col) Formes no1:5-6 D 1929.
A slightly altered translation appears in American Arts Monthly 2no3:14-15 S 1936.

* 131 "MAN'S INHUMANITY TO MAN." 6il Magazine of Art 34:86-7 F 1941.
Exhibition, Phillips Memorial Gallery.

MANUEL, ROLAND. See 74.

132 MARITAIN, JACQUES. Georges Rouault. Revue Universelle 17:505-8 My 15 1924.
Reprinted in part, accompanied by 5il, in Cahiers d'Art 3no3:97-100 1928. Reprinted with supplementary text in the author's Frontières de la poésie. p127-39 Paris, L. Rouart, 1935, the English translation of which was
* published under title Art and poetry. p22-9 New York, Philosophical library, 1943.

133 MARITAIN, RAÏSSA. Les grandes amitiés: souvenirs. p220-8 New York, Éditions de la Maison Française, 1941.
English translation in the author's We have been friends together. p157-63 New York, Longmans, Green, 1942. An excerpt with 3il
* appears in Art News 40:14,27-8 D 15 1941.

* 134 MASTER OF BLACK. Art Digest 14:20 My 15 1940.
Exhibition, Buchholz Gallery.

* 135 MASTER OF BLACK. 1il Art Digest 13:25 O 1 1938.
Exhibition, Museum of Modern Art.

* 136 MATISSE, PIERRE, GALLERY, NEW YORK. A selection of early paintings, water colors, tempera paintings and gouaches from the year nineteen hundred and four to the year nineteen hundred and seventeen by Georges Rouault. 2p 9il por 1937.
Exhibition catalog.

* 137 —— Paintings by Rouault. folded sheet por [1933]
Exhibition catalog.

138 MELLQUIST, JEROME. Rouault, prophet of disaster. Commonweal 36:390-2 Ag 14 1942.

139 —— Georges Rouault: Christian painter. Commonweal 29:232-4 D 23 1938.

140 MONK'S MYTHS. 1il Time 32:43-4 O 3 1938.
Exhibition, Museum of Modern Art.

* 141 NEUMANN, J. B., ed. Georges Rouault, Munich exhibition, 1930. 5p 33il New York-München, J. B. Neumann and G. Franke, 1930. (Artlover library, 4)
Preface by Will Grohmann.
—— See also 96.

* 142 NEUMANN, J. B., GRAPHISCHES KABINETT, MUNICH. Rouault Ausstellung . . . 4p 1il 1930.
    Text by Waldemar George.

* 143 NEW ART CIRCLE, NEW YORK. Etchings by Rouault published by Ambroise Vollard. 15p 15il [1926] (Artlover: J. B. Neumann's Bilderhefte).
    Illustrations only.

* 144 NEW YORK. MUSEUM OF MODERN ART. Painting in Paris from American collections [ed. by Alfred H. Barr, Jr.] p38-9 2il 1930.

* 145 —— The prints of Georges Rouault [by] Monroe Wheeler. 10p 19il 1938.
    Issued in connection with exhibition held at Museum of Modern Art.

* 146 —— 20th century portraits, by Monroe Wheeler. p16-17,69,81,142 3il 1942.

* 147 NEW YORK VIEWS SMOULDERING ART OF ROUAULT. 1il Art Digest 14:6 My 15 1940.
    Exhibition, Bignou Gallery.

* 148 O'CONNOR, JOHN, JR. The Old King, painting by Georges Rouault purchased . . . for the permanent collection. 1il por Carnegie Magazine 14:99-102 S 1940.

* 149 —— The prints of Georges Rouault. 2il Carnegie Magazine 14:300-3 Mr 1941.

* 150 P., E. H. . . Smith College holds a loan exhibition of Rouault's work. 1il Art News 34:8 N 23 1935.

* 151 PACH, WALTER. Georges Rouault. 2il Parnassus 5:9-11 Ja 1933.

* 152 —— Queer thing, painting. passim por New York, Harper, 1938.
    PELLERIN, JEAN. See 45.

153 PORTFOLIO OF MODERN TAPESTRIES. Fortune 14:75-82 Jy 1936.
    Tapestry made from design by Rouault, p81.

* 154 PUY, MICHEL. L'effort des peintres modernes. p125 Paris, A. Messein, 1933.
    First published in the author's Le dernier état de la peinture. Paris, Le Feu, 1910.

* 155 —— G. Rouault et son oeuvre. 63p 27il Paris, Gallimard, 1920. (Les peintres français nouveaux, no8)
    "Extraits des écrits de Georges Rouault" p15-16.

156 REID, ALEX. & LEFEVRE, LTD., LONDON. The tragic painters. p12-13 1il 1938.

157 RIVIÈRE, JACQUES. Exposition Georges Rouault [Galerie Druet]Nouvelle Revue Française 3:537-8 Ap 1910.
    Reprinted in the author's Études. p52-5 Paris, Éditions de la Nouvelle Revue Française, 1924.

158 ROGER-MARX, CLAUDE. L'oeuvre gravé de Georges Rouault. 3il Byblis p93-100 Autumn 1931.
    Includes quotation from a poem by Rouault.

† 158a ROUAULT. il Le Point 5no26-7:1-80 Ag-O 1943.
    Special issue with articles by Rouault, Léon Lehmann, Jacques Laprade, and George Besson.

* 159 ROUAULT AND THE MIDDLE AGES SPIRIT. 1il London Studio 16(Studio 116):167-8 S 1938.
    Exhibition, Leicester Galleries.

* 160 ROUAULT ETCHINGS. Art News 31:5 My 6 1933.
    Exhibition, Julien Levy Gallery.

* 161 ROUAULT EXHIBITION . . . BIGNOU AND BUCHHOLZ. New Yorker My 18 1940.

* 162 ROUAULT FEATURES LANDMARKS OF MODERN ART. 1il Art Digest 15:8 Ja 15 1941.
    Exhibition, Pierre Matisse Gallery.

* 163 ROUAULT: PIERRE MATISSE GALLERY. 1il Art News 32:5 O 28 1933.
    Exhibition, Pierre Matisse Gallery.

* 164 ROUAULT IN REVIEW. Art Digest 15:13 N 15 1940.
    Exhibition, Boston Institute of Modern Art.

* 165 ROUAULT LITHOGRAPHS. Art News 29:12 N 1 1930.
    Exhibition, New Art Center (J. B. Neumann).

* 166 ROUAULT OF THE "STAINED GLASS" QUALITY. 1il Art Digest 12:13 N 15 1937.
    Exhibition, Pierre Matisse Gallery.

* 167 ROUAULT'S MESSAGE. 1il Art Digest 16:25 N 1 1941.
    Exhibition, Guy E. Mayer Galleries.

* 168 ROUAULT'S RELIGION. Art Digest 15:15 D 1 1940.
    Digest of criticism of Rouault exhibition at Boston Institute of Modern Art.

* 169 ROUAULT RETROSPECTIVE PROVIDES NEW YORK WITH STAR ATTRACTION. 2il Art Digest 15:10 Ap 15 1941.
    Exhibition, Marie Harriman Gallery (New York showing of Boston Institute exhibition).

170 ROULET, CLAUDE. Le peintre français: Georges Rouault: textes inédits et notes d'étude. 30p 2il Neuchâtel, Delachaux et Niestlé, 1937.
    Includes "Soliloques" and "Notes sur la peinture" by Georges Rouault, and bibliographical note.
    —— See also 21.

171 SALMON, ANDRÉ. L'art vivant. p30-2 Paris, Crès, 1920. (Artistes d'hier et d'aujourd'hui)

* 172 —— La jeune peinture française. p30-2 Paris, Société des Trente, A. Messein, 1912.

173 —— Le Miserere de Georges Rouault. 12il Amour de l'Art 6:182-6 My 1925.

174 SERTAT, RAOUL. Le salon des Champs-Elysées. Revue Encyclopédique; recueil documentaire universel et illustré. p185-90 My 15 1895.
    "M. Rouault," p187-8.

* 175 SMITH COLLEGE MUSEUM OF ART, NORTHAMPTON, MASS. Georges Rouault: paintings, lithographs. 5p 1il 1935.
Exhibition catalog.

176 SPEAIGHT, ROBERT. Homage to Rouault. Dublin Review 209:59-68 Jy 1941.
Includes quotations from Rouault's writings.

177 SUARÈS, ANDRÉ. Lettre d'André Suarès à Georges Rouault. Art et les Artistes 20(ns13): 217-18 Ap 1926.
Appears also in Rouault's Souvenirs intimes, p7-9 (bibl.22).

178 —— Rouault. Nouvelle Revue Française 54:389-91 Mr 1940.

* 179 SWEENEY, JAMES JOHNSON. Carnegie International 1938. 1il Parnassus 10:15 N 1938.
Comparison of Rouault's Three Judges with Hofer's The Wind.

* 180 —— Georges Rouault. Parnassus 11:21 Ap 1939.
Exhibition, Pierre Matisse Gallery.

* 181 TERRASSE, CHARLES. French painting in the XXth century. p38 3il(1col) London [etc.] Hyperion press, 1939.
Also published in French under title: La peinture française au XXe siècle.

* 182 —— Georges Rouault. 8il Art d'Aujourd'hui p5-6, Spring 1928.
Includes verse by Rouault.

* 183 THÉOTE, DANIEL. Intimate moments with Rouault: three wars. 17il Tricolor 1no2:65-96 My 1944.
Includes statements by Rouault, facsimile of his handwriting and reproductions of unpublished works.

THIEME-BECKER. See 102.

* 184 UCKERMAN, P. D'. L'art dans la vie moderne. p60-1,75 4il Paris, Flammarion, 1937.

* 185 UPTON, MELVILLE. Prints reveal Rouault's art. 1il New York Sun, O 1 1938.
Exhibition, Museum of Modern Art.

186 VANDERPYL, FRITZ R. Peintres de mon époque. p141-50 Paris, Stock, 1931.

187 VAUXCELLES, LOUIS. La Licorne . . . organise une exposition Rouault. 1il Amour de l'Art 1:243-4 1920.

188 —— Rouault. 4il Carnet des Artistes 10:9-14 Je 15 1917.

* 189 VENTURI, LIONELLO. Georges Rouault. 76p 192il(3 col) New York, E.Weyhe, 1940.
Includes bibliography.

* 190 —— Rouault. 8il Parnassus 11:4-13 O 1939.
—— See also 40.

191 VLAMINCK, MAURICE DE. Désobéir. p126-8 Paris, Corrêa, 1936.

* 192 VOLLARD, AMBROISE. Recollections of a picture dealer. passim 2il Boston, Little, Brown, 1936.
Also published in French under title: Souvenirs d'un marchand de tableaux. Paris, Michel, 1937.

* 193 WATSON, FORBES. [Paintings by Georges Rouault] The Arts 16:578-9 Ap 1930.
Exhibition, Brummer Gallery.

WHEELER, MONROE. See 145, 146.

194 WILENSKI, REGINALD HOWARD. Georges Rouault. 4il Apollo 11:473-4 Je 1930.
Exhibition, St. George's Gallery.

* 195 —— Modern French painters. passim 3il New York, Reynal & Hitchcock, 1940.

* 196 ZAHAR, MARCEL. Georges Rouault; or, the return to the dramatic grotesque. 5il Formes no31:354-5 1933.
On Rouault's woodcuts for Vollard's Les Réincarnations du Père Ubu.

* 197 ZERVOS, CHRISTIAN. Histoire de l'art contemporain. p139-46 7il Paris, Editions "Cahiers d'Art," 1938.

* 198 —— Illustrations de Georges Rouault pour "Les Réincarnations du Père Ubu" de A. Vollard. 3il Cahiers d'Art 7no1-2:66-8 1932.

NOTES RECEIVED FROM THE ARTIST FEBRUARY, 1945

Without assuming the attitude of the figures David painted in his Tennis Court Oath, *let me give briefly my pictorial confession of faith. It will lack the abundant and valuable nuances which I would need more space to develop.*

I must say, although not boasting too much about it, that I have practiced this often legendary art with more or less luck; I have respected a certain internal order and laws which I hope are traditional; removed from passing fashions and contemporaries—critics, artists or dealers—I believe I have kept my spiritual liberty.

* * *

The twisted little man with the broken nose (Michelangelo), tells us that "every noble art is devout"; our own Poussin, sometimes judged a little pompous by certain green youths of my generation who are very much attached to Impressionism and have profited and benefited from it more than the originators themselves, does he not speak of noble, mute art? A certain classical perfume emanates from his works. I used to go and revisit them in the almost deserted halls (of the Louvre) around 1895, on Sunday promenades with our good animateur, Gustave Moreau.

* * *

Durand-Ruel, Sagot and Vollard devoted themselves to what is called "modern art"; other galleries had a window on the boulevards for the "Heather" of Didier-Pouget, for Roybet's men in plumed casques and Vibert's bishops. On a sidestreet one might see in another window of the same shop the condemned who were named: Seurat, van Gogh, Gauguin or Cézanne. A discreet and reticent man, with the face of a good medieval devil of the cathedrals, did the honors for you. His name was Fénéon.

* * *

Being self-taught, I regret appearing a little obscure sometimes because I am ignorant of this literary art in which so many Frenchmen have been honored with a certain secret, blessed gift. . . .

In saying so I think, too, of the gentle smile of Rheims even when mutilated, of our Jeanne's replies to her judges or of her death at the stake, and of many sufferings present today.

* * *

Of all criticisms, of judgments more or less enlightened, biased or rash, of all miseries and vanities of the moment, there remains a mute though sometimes eloquent witness. I mean the poor fragment of canvas or paper before which our contemporaries and those to follow will sing "Halleluiah" or else "Miserere," sometimes without having any idea of the conditions under which the creator may have been constrained to work.

* * *

The following is somewhat anecdotal, to give color to this rather austere text.

In the last war I had the good fortune to be able to point out to Ambroise Vollard an empty house. At l'Isle sur le Serein, where I was staying with my large family, he had sent to me a long telegram asking refuge for his pictures. This was at the moment of the break-through on the Hindenburg Line. After an extremely difficult journey, the details of which would be too long and tiresome here, we arrived at last at Saumur, after endless waits in stations—by day and night, for nobody wanted us in the jammed hotels because we were too many.

I thus had the joy of keeping until the end of the 1914–18 war no less than 70 packages, the works of Cézanne, Gauguin, Degas, Renoir.

I still remember the Three Skulls *by Cézanne and also some Renoir sanguine draw-ings—very large—of which Vollard used to say (wasn't he exaggerating a bit?) that if he had not taken them away from Renoir, the artist would have used them to light his fire. Once the paintings themselves were executed, Renoir considered these large preparatory studies to be somewhat negligible.*

Should I confess that the most Ubu-esque moments of my life, so to speak, (a life certainly more agitated than one would think) were my meetings in certain bookish and other barbed-wire entanglements with Ambroise Vollard. My children, seeing me pass one day with Vlaminck, Derain and Vollard along the rue Lafitte where he had his shop, could well cry: "You appeared to be their little child."

130

At Saumur, then, on a certain profound night it was the little child that girded the giant who would probably have fractured his skull or broken a limb because they had forgotten to affix a chain across a very deep opening leading to the station platform, and he would have plunged into this abyss.

The final point of the adventure was that the next day, some Cézannes having been put down for a minute while we got the tickets, a dog, as ill luck would have it, lifted a leg. Vollard jumped with indignation, not upon the dog, but upon the station-master, who was passing by, and asked with fiery eyes if a dog should have permitted himself this sacrilege. To which the other man, running toward an incoming train full of American soldiers, at least found time to reply breathlessly: "Why not ask me for the moon!"

* * *

If I go back to my first childhood, I see myself armed with a piece of chalk, sketching large heads on the kitchen tiles or on the parquet floor of the old apartment of my grandfather, Alexandre Champdavoine, which faced the Musée Carnavalet, *rue de Sévigné, in Paris, my home territory.*

Heads larger than nature, why? "Why?" Grock, the old clown, would say lowering his voice. What do I know about it myself?

Perhaps quite simply to give pleasure to grandfather who loved the fine arts—but outside of official circles.

He loved Courbet, with his magnificent gifts for painting, who ended his life at La Chaux de Fond in Switzerland, ruined and exiled, after having allegedly knocked down the Vendôme column.

He loved Manet and talked to me of the Dead Toreador—(*I found among some old papers an invitation from Manet to see in his studio the works refused by the official Salon*).

My grandfather died when I was about fifteen. He was my sole spiritual support until Gustave Moreau. I was only thirty when Moreau died. Then there was a desert to cross, and painting: the oasis or the mirage? Well knowing that I knew nothing—having certainly learned quite a bit between twenty and thirty, but considering that I perhaps did not know the essential thing which is to strip oneself, *if that grace is accorded us after having learned much.*

And yet?

Is it not dangerous to talk this way to green youths?

Are they not capable of falsifying the facts of the problem and of believing themselves able to begin where one must end and sometimes conclude?

Am I not myself often impatient, too, and in a hurry to come to a conclusion?

Our old masters started out very young generally and did not pursue two hares at one time. Having produced their masterwork early in the guilds, they possessed the means to express themselves very young, having sometimes begun by grinding colors in the master's studio while still children.

In order to have a taste for enriching the mind, it is perhaps not necessary to be a graduate or have a degree or to be a mandarin with mother-of-pearl buttons.

They once brought me a child who used to cut out with scissors the silhouettes of animals he had just seen at the zoo. When I told the mother, who was of good bourgeois family, that this child should be placed with a sculptor if the bent continued, she replied: "He must first know and learn all that one must know in our world." That was perhaps putting off to a distant time the culmination of a fortunate gift.

It is not the worldly eclecticism of multiple knowledge that enriches, but perseverance in a favorable furrow and the loving, silent effort of a whole life.

False Michelangelos or Leonardos in the making or Raphaels who have scarcely the gift or breadth of a Chardin follower—these think themselves absolutely capable of one day bestowing upon us a new Last Judgment. *If they do not achieve it, they die of vexation.*

That is why I sometimes tremble with sacred anger, may I say, when I am compared in my various attempts with some of the great old masters whom I love . . . I am so far away from them—in a certain way. But can we not say, here more than ever, to make ourselves better understood if possible with regard to this cult of the old masters:

"The letter killeth and the spirit giveth life."   G. R.

Ten thousand copies of this book have been printed in February 1945 for the Trustees of The Museum of Modern Art by The Plantin Press, New York. The color inserts have been printed by William E. Rudge's Sons, New York.